THE WAGGIES

Awards for Dogs Who Love to Hike

I0087302

DOUG GELBERT

illustrations by
ANDREW CHESWORTH

HIKEWITHYOURDOG.COM BOOKS

There is always a new trail to look forward to...

The Waggies: Awards for Dogs Who Love to Hike

hikewithyourdog.com books
a division of Cruden Bay Books

International Standard Book Number   978-1-935771-45-6

Introducing The Waggies

"They look like they are having the time of their lives."
If you hike with dogs chances are you have heard words like that from other trail users when they see your happy trail dogs. Dogs are happy on any trail but they become especially excited on new trails. New scents to sniff. New sounds to hear. New sights to see.

It seems like every group has its own awards these days. So we created the Waggies to honor the best hikes you can take with your dog in America. The nominees are egalitarian, all day hikes that can be reached by driving in the continental United States, just about always in a two-wheel drive vehicle.

Doug Gelbert is our expert selector in awarding the Waggies. Doug has shepherded the hikewithyourdog.com website since 2001 and started the Hiking With Dogs Facebook group that now has over 35,000 members. He has written over two dozen books on hiking with dogs including *The Canine Hiker's Bible*, *How To Hike With Dogs At Our National Parks - Even When They're Not Allowed On The Trail*, and *300 Day Hikes To Take With Your Dog Before He Tires You Out*.

What about snubs? Of course there will be snubs. Arguing about who has been dissed is the best part of awards shows. Send us in your favorite hikes with your dog for the next round of Waggies. Until then, the envelopes please... and let's start handing out Waggies!

"Dogs are our link to paradise...to sit with a dog on a hillside on a glorious afternoon is to be back in Eden, where doing nothing was not boring - it was peace.
- Milan Kundera

Ahead On The Trail...

Best Canine Hike
In A National Park

Somehow Canada allows dogs on the trail in some of the most magnificent national parks on the planet while handling millions of visitors each year **and** protecting wildlife. Not so in the United States. Rather than dwell on the disaster zone that most American national parks are for dog owners let's move swiftly to the meager list of nominees in this category...

Acadia National Park (Maine)
Great Head Trail

Acadia was the first national park created east of the Mississippi River and the first one that used donated private land. It no doubt helped future canine hikers that it would not have been a good look to ban the dogs of prominent donor families - primarily the dog-loving Rockefellers who brought some the earliest Bullmastiffs to America - from the park. So today there are over 100 miles of foot trails and 45 miles of carriage paths open to dogs at "the Crown Jewel of the North Atlantic Coast." Acadia's *Great Head Trail* delivers those shiny ocean views in a 1.7-mile loop that includes time in a fragrant spruce-fir boreal forest.

Congaree National Park (South Carolina)
Boardwalk Loop

Congaree National Park protects the largest contiguous area of old-growth bottomland hardwood forest remaining in the United States. More than 52 million acres of floodplain forests have been decimated in the southeastern United States in the past century making Congaree's 2,000 acres of virgin pine, tupelo and bald cypress special indeed. The park's forests harbor 20 state or national champion trees including loblolly pines, hickories and bald cypress under one of the highest deciduous roofs in the world. Your dog can enjoy it all, beginning with the marquee 2.4-mile *Boardwalk Loop* and step down for woodland rambles along the Congaree River.

Cuyahoga Valley National Park (Ohio)
Ledges Trail

Raise your hand if you knew that America's first national park of the 21st Century was created in..............Cleveland? To the first people who came here 12,000 years ago the Cuyahoga was the "crooked river." As befits its history as a recreation destination, Cuyahoga permits dogs on its trails. It doesn't have the feel of the grand American national parks but instead evokes an intimate local park feel that will suite your best trail companion just fine. The *Ledges Trail* highlights the area's unique geology as it circles the imposing rock formations on a wide footpath for over two miles. Spur trails climb to the nooks and crannies and the top of the ledges, often with stone steps to ease your dog's journey.

Grand Canyon National Park (Arizona)
South Rim Trail

This is our only nominee from the great Western national parks so indelibly etched in our imaginations. When Theodore Roosevelt visited as President in 1903 he took his best oratorical shot by saying, "The Grand Canyon fills me with awe. It is beyond comparison - beyond description." He concluded by stating that the handiwork of the Colorado River is "the one great sight which every American should see." Your American dog can indeed see the Grand Canyon but is not allowed below the rim, the grandeur comes from the 14 miles of trail that snakes along the South Rim.

Mammoth Cave National Park (Kentucky)
Green River Bluffs Trail

Not named for extinct wooly elephants, Mammoth Cave earns its chops as the world's longest known cave system with more than 400 miles of passages mapped, so many that the guides like to point out that you could put the second and third longest caves systems inside the limestone labyrinth and have more than 100 miles left over. Your dog will have to be content with the dark hollows and hardwood forests above ground. The *Green River Bluffs Trail* meanders through the thick canopy to a promontory above the eponymous river and ties into a complex of other easy-trotting paths. The route also leads to the Historic Entrance of the great cave that will deliver a blast of cold air onto your curious dog's nose.

And the Waggie for Best Canine Hike In A National Park goes to...

...Acadia National Park!

When you put the Grand Canyon in a category it's awful hard to give the award to anyone else but, hey, Meryl Streep doesn't win every year she's nominated either.

The *Great Head Trail* loops across secluded Sand Beach on Newport Cove - dogs are welcome on the sand and for a dip in the ocean except in the summer - and most canine hikers go right at the head of the loop. But going left into the maritime forest saves the spectacular coastal views from one of America's highest headlands until the end.

This land was once owned by financier J.P. Morgan who gave it to his daughter, Louisa Satterlee. She constructed a stout stone tea house tower in 1915 at the highest point of Great Head, 145 feet above the waves. A fire damaged the tower in 1947 and destroyed three adjacent bungalows so the land was donated to the park shortly afterwards. The remains of the foundation are still seen on the hike.

Lurking above Sand Beach at the beginning is the 520-foot Beehive with its exposed cliffs. The wide path into the forest is paw-friendly as it winds through white birch tree trunks and dark spruce conifers. Once atop the cliffs the going is mostly level with surprises for your dog around every crag as the trail picks its way along blue lines above the crashing ocean. With stops to watch seals and harbor porpoises this stretch of the canine hike can take some time.

Best Canine Hike
on the Seacoast

America's coastal headlands don't generally get as much pub as their neighboring sandy beaches. That is probably because it is a lot easier to hike on level sand than tramp along rocky shores. But tucked along the 12,383 miles of United States coastline are some true gems of seacoast hiking with your dog. The nominees for the best are...

Cape Lookout State Park (Oregon)

The *Cape Lookout Trail* is almost guaranteed to be muddy in spots and you'll realize why when you finish this hike with your dog after almost 2.5 miles. Standing on the smallish opening at the end of the wooded peninsula you will feel as if you are in the center of the Pacific Ocean. Even 400 feet above the crashing water your dog will feel the power of the sea around you. This is just about as close as you can get to migrating gray whales without a boat. Old growth Sitka spruce and western hemlock shelter leathery polypody ferns as the trail rolls along with only modest ups and downs to its thrilling conclusion.

Cliff Walk (Rhode Island)

Newport's "cottages" are America's finest collection of Gilded Age mansions, built on spellbinding rocky bluffs overlooking the Atlantic Ocean. No matter how rich the owner, however, no one's property could extend all the way to the shoreline. By virtue of "Fisherman's Rights," first granted under British colonial rule and then enshrined in the Rhode Island constitution, the public is always guaranteed the legal right to walk along a small sliver of cliff. Hence, America's finest backyard stroll with your dog. At the end of the *Cliff Walk* you will drop to ocean's edge and Reject's Beach where your dog can get in some ocean dog paddling. You now have the option of returning by the same route along the black Atlantic rocks or exiting into the town and walking back on the sidewalks in front of the mansions whose backyards you have just wandered through.

Ecola State Park (Oregon)

There are 363 miles of tail-friendly coastline in Oregon - every bit of it - and this chunk on top of Tillamook Head may be the most dramatic. It was even on Lewis and Clark's radar when the Corps of Discovery chased down rumors of a beached whale here in 1806. "The grandest and most pleasing prospects which my eyes ever surveyed," wrote Captain William Clark. Six miles of trails scour every yard of Tillamook Head but your destination is an *Oregon Coast Trail* Hiking Camp and beyond it a spur to breathtaking views of the Pacific, including the impressively sighted Tillamook Rock Light perched offshore.

Oswald West State Park (Oregon)

Cape Falcon is named for the shape of the headlands and not its diving raptors but you may well spot migrating whales and sea lions in the waters around these cliffs. The canine hike across the peninsula is dominated by massive Sitka spruce trees and offers such dog-pleasing diversions as the cascading Blumenthal Falls and detours to Short Sand Beach and Smuggler's Cove for dog paddling. The woods give way to meadows choked with salal near the end of the canine hike's 2.4-mile journey. Paths cut through the seaside shrubbery lead to a parade of Pacific Ocean viewpoints.

Quoddy Head (Maine)

How would you like to stand with your dog on the easternmost point in the continental United States and experience the nation's first sunrise (at least part of the year, depending on the earth's tilt.) You can do just that at Quoddy Head State Park where a lighthouse guiding ships through the fog has perched on 80-foot black rock cliffs since President Thomas Jefferson signed the authorization papers in 1808. The *Coastal Trail* rolls south from the West Quoddy Head Light for two miles along the clifftops. Your dog will thrill in this rollercoaster romp at land's end, eagerly bounding to the top of the many hillocks to see what awaits on the other side as the path dips and rises. Keep an eye on the waves crashing in from the Atlantic Ocean - tides can fluctuate as much as 20 feet. The final drop is into Carrying Place Cove where dog paddling is a must in the shallow waters lapping onto a sandy beach.

And the Waggie for Best Canine Hike on the Seacoast goes to...

...Cliff Walk!

Can there be a group winner? King Solomon himself couldn't decide among the three Oregon seacoast hikes. But the *Cliff Walk* is no compromise winner. Where else can your dog have more fun hopping on boulders and dodging ocean waves? The first two miles are paved and easy to hike but continuing past the macadam the *Cliff Walk* turns rustic with some walking on unprotected, open cliff faces. It requires concentration but any level of canine hiker can negotiate the trip. It's not unusual to catch a bit of ocean spray on the tail out here. There is plenty of chance for swimming at either end of the hike, on First Beach or Reject's Beach, to cap a spirited day on the Atlantic Seacoast. It is not without reason that the *Cliff Walk* was anointed the first National Recreation Trail in New England.

Best Canine Hike
to a Lighthouse

You don't often hear the word "romantic" tossed around when hiking with your dog but it is inevitable when a lighthouse is on the day's canine hiking menu. Lighthouses fire the imagination for life at sea, gorgeous sunrises or sunsets at the edges of America, and dramatic seascapes captured on canvas. The payoff on a hike to a silent sentinel of the sea is always special indeed. The nominees for the best our coasts have to offer your dog are..

Cape Disappointment State Park (Washington)

The first disappointment at the mouth of the great Columbia River was when British fur trader John Meares was looking for it in 1788 and stopped just miles from the discovery. The second was when the U.s. Army Corps of Engineers built a lighthouse that turned out to be hard to see for ships approaching from the south. It was anything but disappointment in 1805 for Lewis & Clark explorers, including their Newfoundland dog Seaman, saw the Pacific Ocean for the first time at these headlands, culminating a 4,133-mile journey that had begun three years earlier in St. Louis on the Mississippi River. Canine hiking at Cape Disappointment stuffs art, history, old growth forests, a lighthouse, an old army battery, and stunning scenery into a small daypack.

Cape Hatteras National Seashore (North Carolina)

The Outer Banks feature five lighthouses you can visit with your dog. They still haven't prevented more than 600 ships from wrecking on the shoals offshore and earning the long barrier island the moniker "Graveyard of the Atlantic." The most famous of the quintet is America's tallest, the 208-foot black-and-white swirled Cape Hatteras Lighthouse that peeks out over the dunes during a *loooong* hike with your dog down the national seashore. When you arrive, or if you used the short nature trail, your dog will have to wait while you hike the 268 steps inside to the top.

Montauk Point State Park (New York)

In 1792 Congress appropriated $255.12 to buy land upon which a light was to be built to guide boats past the perilous rocks at the eastern end of Long Island. The first whale oil was lit in 1797 in New York's first lighthouse and America's fourth. For millions of immigrants sailing across the Atlantic Ocean the historic Montauk Lighthouse was the first American building they saw. Canine hiking in the shadow of the Light passes Money Pond where pirate Captain Kidd supposedly stashed two treasure chests but no loot has ever been found. Your dog may feel as if they've discovered gold on this tight, twisty route however. The sandy surface is a delight on the paw and the many dips and rolls are certain to pique any dog's interest.

Port Orford Heads State Park (Oregon)

The Oregon coast is one of the great sights in America. Spectacular, but also dangerous. So many ships wrecked off these 280-foot headlands that one of Oregon's first lifeboat stations was built here in the 1930s. The canine hiking is all on top of the headlands and begins in a thick Sitka spruce forest, amidst many impressive specimens of the breed. After a stop at the remains of the old 37-foot observation tower, connect with the *Headland Trail* that picks its way through low-growing conifers and blankets of leathery Western salal shrubs. On the headlands nothing grows high enough that a golden retriever can't see above to the long views out to sea.

Split Rock Lighthouse State Park - (Minnesota)

There are 246 lighthouses, more or less, on the Great Lakes and the light at Split Rock is the most photographed. There were no roads in the area when the squat, octagonal tower was constructed in 1910 so the building materials had to be lifted by crane from the water to the top of the 130-foot volcanic rock cliff. Split Rock was selected as Lake Superior's lighthouse for a series of stamps issued by the United States Postal Service and took a star turn in the 2013 Hollywood version of *The Great Gatsby*. Of course your dog will want to see it. Short trails in the park make that happen - from up close on top of the promontory, from down below along Ellingsen Beach, and on top at Dry Hill. With your camera sated your trail dog will be ready to head out on the spirited five-mile *Split Rock River Loop*.

And the Waggie for Best Canine Hike to a Lighthouse goes to…

…Cape Disappointment State Park!

Start your Waggie Award-winning hike with your dog with some first-rate swimming and fetching in a sandy, driftwood-strewn cove known as Waikiki Beach. Then follow a series of art trails created by Maya Lin of Vietnam Memorial fame for the Confluence Project in 2006. An inscribed boardwalk recounts the adventures of the Lewis and Clark expedition here with quotes from journals. The trail makes a sporty ascent of the Sitka spruce-covered headlands with views of the Pacific Ocean and the Columbia River from grassy outcroppings. The destination is the Cape Disappointment Lighthouse that was built 200 feet above the surf in 1856. Despite its advantageous position, north-sailing ships couldn't see the beacon so a second light tower had to be built on the North Head. Save some time for the hike with your dog there as well.

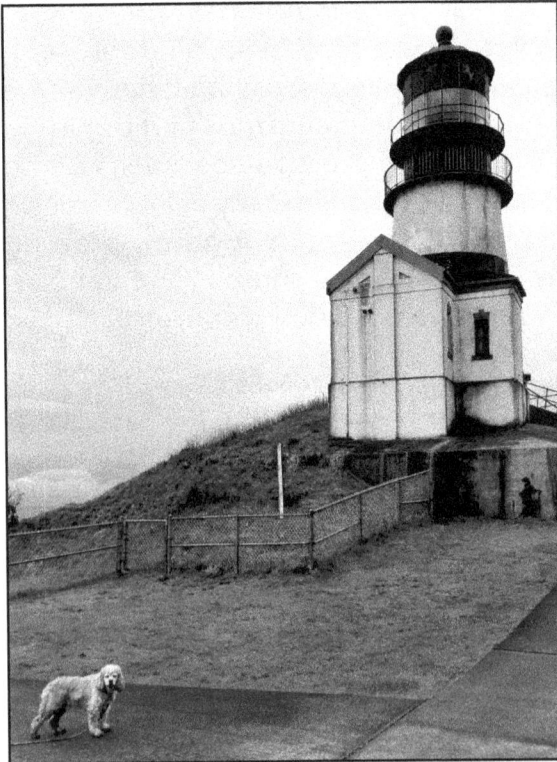

Best Canine Hike
at the Beach (Atlantic Division)

Have you ever noticed how many television and magazine advertisements feature people loving life with their dogs at the beach? Why? Because nothing screams "I'm having a great time" faster than showing dogs at the beach. It may come as quite a surprise to those marketers that half of America's beaches do not allow dogs. Let's hike past those depressing NO DOGS ON BEACH signs double time and start handing out Waggies to tail-friendly sands...

Assateague Island National Seashore (Maryland)

Assateague Island - the sands were connected to the mainland until 1933 when an August hurricane tore open an inlet to the Sinepuxent Bay - is best known for its free-roaming Chincoteague ponies. Legend has it that the original herd escaped a shipwrecked Spanish galleon and swam ashore. The ponies rule the island and your dog is likely to see them on the roads or even meet the mostly oblivious equines in the surf. Once you and your dog start hiking at South Ocean Beach there are miles of undeveloped beach until the Virginia border is reached and dogs are not allowed further. That is the better part of a dozen miles so count on a full day of canine beach hiking at Assateauge on the undeveloped, windswept beach sands.

Cape Cod National Seashore (Massachusetts)

Cape Cod reigns as our most popular national seashore. Where once only fishermen and whalers came, the 40-mile stretch of sand dunes between Chatham and Provincetown at the tip of the cape attract five million visitors a year. In addition to its sandy beaches, dogs are allowed on all non-nesting unprotected beaches year-round. Walking the beaches at Cape Cod is a special experience due to limited sight distance down the shore caused by the coastline's curvature. The effect is that of a series of private beaches as you move from beach alcove to beach alcove. In addition to Atlantic Ocean beaches backed by impressive highlands, the park extends across the cape to include bayside beaches with gentler waves for canine aquatics.

Duck Beach (North Carolina)

If you own a dog who loves to frolic in the waves you know the town of Duck, or you should. Duck is the northernmost incorporated town on the 70 miles of a trio of sandy barrier islands at Cape Hatteras; it sports water frontage on both the Atlantic Ocean and Carrituck Sound. Dogs are allowed to hike down the ocean sands year-round, unleashed. If you have been searching for a beach nirvana for your dog, this is it.

Island Beach State Park (New Jersey)

Yes, there is a barrier island in New Jersey where you can stand with your dog and look out at the Atlantic Ocean without being on a board-walk or a beach house deck. Island Beach State Park protects 10 miles of dunesland that have survived virtually untouched as they have always been. There are a series of short nature trails (less than one mile) as you drive down the main park road to its end at Barnegat Inlet but once your dog gets that whiff of salt air in their nose, they may not be in any mood to tarry. Get to the beach! This is one of the few places in New Jersey you can enjoy the Atlantic Ocean with your dog in the summer. The only catch is parking is limited and the park shuts down if you get your dog to the sand too late.

Jekyll Island State Park (Georgia)

America's richest families (enough titans of industry wintered here that it was once estimated that one-sixth of all the world's wealth was represented on Jekyll Island), today the entire island, including 11 miles of Atlantic Ocean beach, is a state park. The beaches around Jekyll Point at the south end are undeveloped and your dog can hike for hours beside natural wind-sculpted dunes. There is ocean swimming and bay swimming - your dog's choice. The northern nob of the island juts into Saint Simons Sound and the sands are harder and the surf gentler; Driftwood Beach here is one of the best beach hikes you will ever take with your dog.

"And sometimes when you'd get up in the middle of the night
you'd hear the reassuring thump, thump of her tail on the floor,
letting you know that she was there and thinking of you."
-William Cole

And the Waggie for Best Canine Hike at the Beach (Atlantic Division) goes to...

...Jekyll Island State Park!

Driftwood Beach takes home the Waggie with something no Atlantic Ocean beach has to offer - an art sculpture garden. Unlike a museum's sculptures your dog can climb on these twisted and beautiful works of art and play to their heart's content. Jekyll Island is Georgia's smallest barrier island and Driftwood Beach at the remote northern end - just across from the dog-friendly campground - isn't big but expect to spends hours walking with your dog through the arboreal graveyard of sun-bleached fallen oaks and pines. The weathered trees were sent to the shoreline by erosion and left in their natural decaying state, just waiting for your fun-loving dog.

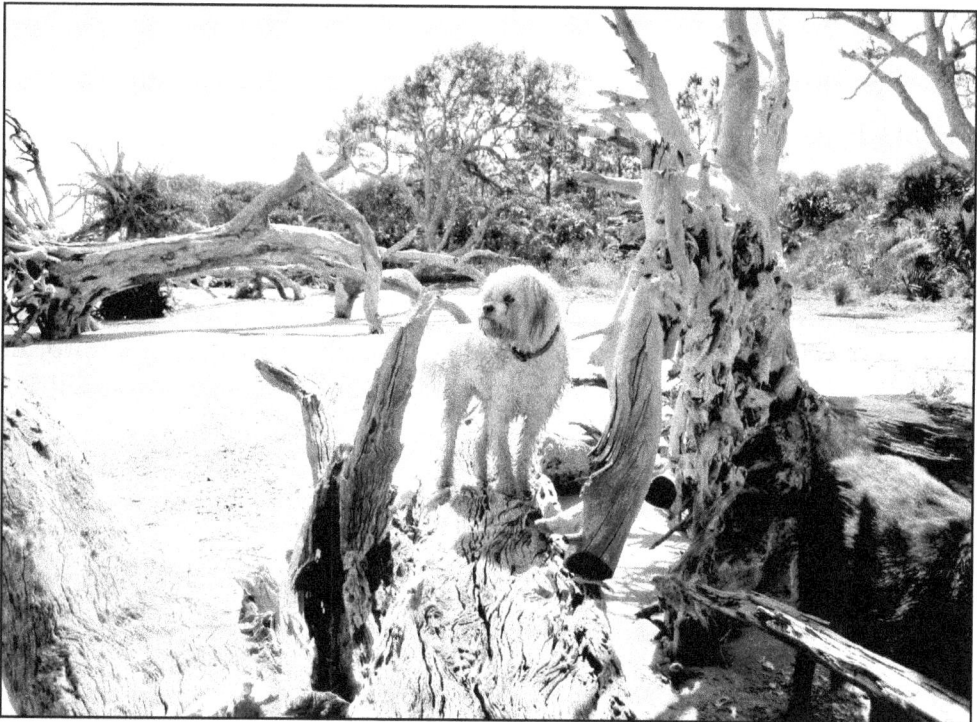

Best Canine Hike
at the Beach (Gulf Coast Division)

The hundreds of miles of Gulf of Mexico beaches are known for their soft sugar sands, clear waters, and both sunsets and sunrises but not so much for being friendly to dogs. Nonetheless, one of these beaches will claim the Waggie...

Dauphin Island Park & Beach (Alabama)

Alabama's lone barrier island was fortified to protect Mobile Bay in 1821, just two years after the Yellowhammer State was admitted to the Union. Fort Gaines and Fort Morgan across the entrance to the bay remained active until 1923. Afterwards Dauphin Island morphed into a resort destination. The wild West End Beach is private and doesn't allow dogs but the Public Beach across the southern heart of the island offers miles of dog-friendly hiking past beach houses, a quiet cove, sandy spits, and dune-backed sand.

Grand Isle State Park (Louisiana)

Louisiana's only inhabited barrier island once attracted the likes of pirate captain Jean Lafitte and his band of salty sea dogs. Nature seems to not favor Grand Isle's cadre of some 1,400 permanent residents - the island takes more punches from than just about any other beach in America. A hurricane arrives, on average, every three years. This century alone Isidore, Lili, Cindy, Katrina, Rita, and Gustav all have visited. Today's "Sportsman's Paradise" is known for its world-class fishing and birding. Beach houses line the miles of Gulf sand but are on bluffs far enough back from the shore to give this hike with your dog a naturalistic feeling. Grand Isle tilts just enough to the northeast for splendid beach sunrises.

Honeymoon Island (Florida)

Honeymoon Island is the best place to hike with your dog along the Gulf of Mexico on the Florida peninsula. The island was cleaved from a larger island by the Hurricane of 1921 and purchased by Tampa entrepreneur Clinton Washburn. The undeveloped island had been used to raise hogs but the new proprietor cooked up a scheme with *Life* magazine in 1940 for a contest to win Florida honeymoons. Thatched bungalows were hurriedly built and 164 enraptured couples enjoyed all-expenses-paid nuptial trips before World War II intervened and that was it for the newlyweds. Today the *Osprey Trail* runs up the spine of a sand spit for over one mile, working through one of Florida's last old growth slash pine forests; some trees are almost 200 years old. It is all easy trotting for your dog on a mixture of grass and sand under paw.

Padre Island National Seashore (Texas)

Everything is bigger in Texas. It just is. That includes the world's longest undeveloped barrier island. Your dog can romp for over 65 miles and see nothing but surf and dunes. Malaquite Beach is the main vehicle-free area on Padre Island. For less communal hiking with your dog head to South Beach where the first five miles of sand are suitable for all vehicles. Beyond that the primitive beach sand turns soft. Seaman can find quite an array of curiosities on this hike as anything tossed into the Gulf of Mexico, including objects from offshore gas platforms, eventually washes up here.

St. George Island State Park (Florida)

You can just about count the number of Florida panhandle Gulf of Mexico beaches that welcome dogs on one paw. St. George Island, a narrow 22-mile strip of sand that creates oyster-rich Apalachicola Bay, is one of those places so you can be sure many dog owners are making their way across the Bryant G. Patton Bridge to the park where nine miles of beaches and dunes have been spared from development. The bayside beach is studded with photogenic ghost trees and a few surviving arboreal warriors still waging the good fight at land's end. All provide perches for a variety of seabirds and ample ammunition for a game of fetch in the Gulf of Mexico before retracing the sandy pawprints to the trailhead.

And the Waggie for Best Canine Hike at the Beach (Gulf Coast Division) goes to…

…Dauphin Island Park & Beach!

Timing is everything. The sand spit hike that wins Dauphin Island the Waggie didn't even exist a decade ago and may well be gone in another ten years. The unique geology that created the Pelican Peninsula that juts for one mile south into the Gulf of Mexico only occurs every 150 years or so. But while it is here this unique canine beach hike permits a rare oceanside loop completely on seashell-speckled sand. Someday the Pelican Peninsula will be an island once more and the wooden fishing pier that now ends on sand 250 yards from the water will once again have lines cast over the side. Until that time enjoy the morning sunrises and evening sunsets while walking your dog on the sandy spit at Dauphin Island.

Best Canine Hike
at the Beach (Pacific Division)

California is decidedly a mixed bag for dogs at the beach, Oregon allows dogs on all of its 363 miles of shoreline, and dogs are generally a go on Washington beaches. So let's see the nominees for best Pacific Ocean beach hike with your dog...

Cannon Beach (Oregon)

Miles of wide, flat sand beaches will certainly thrill your dog but that isn't enough for this paw-friendly paradise to be named one of the 100 most beautiful places in the world by National Geographic, as Cannon Beach was in 2013. No, it was the collection of photogenic sea stacks on the shoreline that cinched that designation. Most prominent is Haystack Rock; one of the largest free-standing rocks on the planet at 235 feet tall. At low tide your dog can trot right up to the monolith and smell the sea creatures clinging to its sides. Even without the sea stacks Cannon Beach delivers one of the longest beach hikes on the Oregon coast.

Carmel-by-the-Sea (California)

The Basilica of Mission San Carlos Borromeo del Rio Carmel was the second mission built in California, founded in Monterey in 1770 and moved to its present location by Spanish mis- sionaries a year later. Artists discovered the village in the early 1900s and strict zoning ordinances keep Carmel, only one mile square, a town of eclectic cottages and bungalows. Luckily, those strict laws don't extend to dogs - you will never find a more dog-friendly beach than Carmel where dogs and people mingle freely, neither constrained with leashes.

Los Padres National Forest (California)

Thanks to Pfeiffer Beach Seaman does not have to settle with seeing Big Sur, where dogs are almost universally banned from trails and beaches, only from the car window. Pfeiffer Beach is a place where the word "magical" is tossed around as easily as "good dog" at a puppy training class. The sand is wrapped in spectacular rock formations making Pfeiffer Beach a very secluded place indeed. Offshore, Keyhole Rock, a natural arch where surf blasts through, frames an evening sunset. The rocky coves make for frisky waves and exciting play in the waves for dogs. Extended canine beach hiking is available to the north, tides permitting.

Meyers Creek Beach (Oregon)

Your dog may recognize Meyers Creek Beach from its many star turns in television commercials. Or maybe from its frequent hosting of the Windsurfing World Championship. The same sea stacks that define Cannon Beach create some of America's most scenic oceanfront on these sands. Here, however, the giant rocks actually seem to be invading the beach from the sea. Your dog will have to negotiate around the phalanx of sea stacks while hiking down the beach. Meyers Creek snakes its way through the sand and out into the Pacific Ocean to deliver even more photographic punch here.

Olympic National Park - Ruby Beach (Washington)

You are never going to hike with your dog on another beach like Kalaloch (CLAY-lock). When the sea gets angry it disgorges massive logs onto the shores of the most remote northwestern part of the country. Thousands upon thousands of logs. Seven ocean beaches feature short jaunts through the coastal rain forest from adjoining Highway 101 - six with numbers and Ruby Beach. Your dog will take less than ten minutes to reach the sand from the bluffs but this won't be any ordinary beachcombing expedition - there is plenty of stepping to be done on and around, on top, and across these piles of bleached elephantine driftwood in the soft sand. Ruby Beach is a bit pebblier under paw than its cousins but also features more dramatic sea stacks in the surf. Your dog can hike right up to the rock formations and little Abbey Island at low tide - the only time you want to enjoy these beaches since the waves can crash right up to the bluffs in places. Long canine beach hikes are possible north and south if you know the tides.

"No one appreciates the very special genius
of your conversation as a dog does."
-Christopher Morley

And the Waggie for Best Canine Hike at the Beach (Pacific Division) goes to...

...Carmel-by-the-Sea!

Carmel is the model for the way dogs should be allowed to enjoy a beach and that makes these soft sands a shoo-in for a Waggie. This is the biggest beach among the craggy headlands of the spectacular Monterey Peninsula. To your north will be the world-famous 18th hole of the Pebble Beach Golf Links and to your south the beach is framed by dramatic cliffs. Straight ahead will be mesmerizing views of Monterey Bay. Spanning from Carmel Beach to Carmel River Beach, your dog can trot down the hard-packed Scenic Road path with forever memories around every turn. Oh, and bring plenty of treats to hand out for all the new dog friends you'll meet along your hike.

Best Canine Hike In Sand Dunes (Shore Division)

Between development and landscape-altering storms it is a chore to keep a good dune system on America's coasts. The shore dunes can't compete with their inland cousins in majesty but they are not lacking in rollicking doggie fun. Let's see the nominees for hiking with your dog through dunes where the sand meets the sea...

Indiana Dunes State Park (Indiana)

Indiana celebrated its first national park with the elevation of Indiana National Seashore to top dog status in 2019. Dog owners in the know, however, check in at the trailhead in Indiana Dunes State Park next door where the three tallest dunes in the Hoosier State reside. A 1.5-mile 3 Dune Challenge conquers Mount Jackson (elevation 176 feet), Mount Holden (184 feet), and Mount Tom (192 feet). Wooden stairs are a big help. Prepare your dog for 40-degree slopes on the edge of Lake Michigan.

Jockey's Ridge State Park (North Carolina)

Jockey's Ridge, with heights varying from 80 to 100 feet, is the tallest natural sand dune system on the Atlantic seacoast. Once discovered, the naked hilltops served as an important navigational landmark for European explorers. Its name is thought to survive from pony races staged in the flats at the base of the dune. All of the sand mountains are open to exploration but interpretive trails are staked across the dunes for structure. The Atlantic Ocean is seen but not accessible; the sands do run down to the calm waters of Roanoke Sound for a doggie dip or a cooling sandy walk through the shallows.

Jonathan Dickinson State Park (Florida)

Quaker merchant Jonathan Dickinson shipwrecked on the Atlantic coast here in 1696 and the colorful history since then has included a secretive military base and a roadside tourist legend known as the "Wildman of the Loxachatchee." The ancient dunes are not open sand but are covered with pine scrub which is regularly drubbed by the elements. Hiking on the *East Loop Trail* delivers some of the highest hills and longest views in South Florida. The canine hiking day can be stretched to many hours off the dunes and ties into the fabled *Florida Trail*.

Oregon Dunes National Recreation Area (Oregon)

This is the Super Bowl of doggie sand play with 40 miles of tail-friendly beach. The mountains of sand at Oregon Dunes are the tallest on the Pacific Coast and extend inland for 2.5 miles. Canine hikers here cross open oblique dunes, pristine interdune lakes, peaceful lagoons, and beautiful tree islands. From the top of a dune there are long views through the intermittent forest out to the Pacific Ocean, the ultimate destination on this spectacular hike with your dog.

Sleeping Bear Dunes National Lakeshore (Michigan)

In 2011 the ABC morning program *Good Morning America* anointed Sleeping Bear Dunes the "Most Beautiful Place in America." A park, especially one with 400-foot high lakeside dunes, can live off that type of publicity for a long time. The *Cottonwood Trail* is the place to stop on the scenic drive and get out of your vehicle to hike with your dog. This is a rollicking rollercoaster of a canine hike and even though it is only 1.4 miles you are working through thick sand all the way. The loop leads out into dunes speckled with the bleached remains of over-whelmed trees and the hardy survivors adapting to their sand-immer-sive world. The tenaciousness of these trees to provide occasional shade and resting areas is welcome indeed.

"Dog. A kind of additional or subsidiary Deity
designed to catch the overflow and surplus of the world's worship."
-Ambrose Bierce

And the Waggie for Best Canine Hike In Sand Dunes (Shore Division) goes to...

...Oregon Dunes National Recreation Area!

When the big dog wants to eat everyone else moves aside and so the largest expanse of coastal sand dunes in North America takes home this Waggie. The tallest reach 500 feet in height. Where those dunes end at Tahkenitch Creek is where some of the best canine hiking in the recreation area kicks off. Four staked trails poke into the dunes with a loop of over six miles possible on the *Tahkenitch Dunes* and *Threemile Lake North* trails. The creek adds personality to this sandy trek as it carves a sinuous path to the Pacific Ocean and the islands of coastal pines break up the shimmering piles of sand. Take the the dunes trail first when everyone is fresh and save the lake trail that travels through the lush deciduous forest for the end. If there wasn't enough dog-paddling on the beach there is more swimming available in Elbow Lake.

Best Canine Hike
In Sand Dunes (Inland Division)

Do dogs have more fun racing in nature's sand box than anywhere else? It sure seems like it when dog meets dunes. America is not lacking for opportunities for your dog to shift into four-paw drive and climb massive piles of sand. So without further delay let's meet the nominees for the best place for sandy hikes away from the shore...

Bruneau Dunes State Park (Idaho)

Unlike its sister dune fields across western America, Bruneau Dunes is the site of the country's highest single-structured sand dune. Sands have accumulated in a natural basin since the Bonneville Flood inundated this terrain 15,000 years ago. Prevailing winds blow in opposite directions about equal amounts of time and so, unlike most dunes, these do not drift far. The Bruneau Dunes rise approximately 470 feet. You are free to climb anywhere; as a bonus the dunes back to a small desert lake waiting to refresh a tired sand-climbing dog. Hardy canine adventurers will want to jump on the *Dunes 5-Mile Hiking Trail* that follows a circular path in semi-wilderness desert terrain, crossing dunesland and marshland.

Coral Pink Sand Dunes State Park (Utah)

The same iron oxides and minerals that produce the color in Utah's Mighty Five national parks are responsible for the coral-colored Navajo sandstone that has eroded and blown into this notch in the mountains over thousands of years where the winds are pinched so much they can't sustain enough speed to carry away the grains of sand. The *Two Dunes Trail* visits a wind-blown barchan (crescent- shaped dune) and a star-shaped dune caused by winds coming from several directions before returning in less than two miles. The Coral Pink Sand Dunes work their magic best on early morning hikes before the off-road crowd is permitted in at 9:00 a.m.

Great Sand Dunes National Park and Preserve (Colorado)

The tallest sand dunes in North America formed here when sand from ancient dry lake beds got trapped in a low curve of the Sangre de Cristo Mountains. Prevailing winds from the valley floor blow toward the mountains but frequent storm winds blow the dunes back into the valley. This opposing wind action causes the sand to pile up vertically in the natural pocket. There are no designated trails in the park sand and your dog is invited to explore to the top of the first ridge of the 30-square mile dunefield, the imposing "High Dune" which affords a 360-degree view from its 650-foot summit. Medano Creek trickles down from the mountains to cool the sands - and paws - at the head of the dunes.

Mojave National Preserve - Kelso Dunes (California)

Don't be put off by the Devil's Playground that is anchored by the Kelso Dune Field - these stacked dunes are easy to reach and fun to climb. The tallest top out at about 650 feet and there are long hikes available along the crest. Oddly, the sand here is not being replenished so your dog is hiking on grains that have been around a long time. If you slide down Kelso Dunes slowly the sand will begin to "sing." Your dog will probably take a pass on that.

White Sands National Monument (New Mexico)

When America's space age began at White Sands Missile Range with the firing of a Tiny Tim test booster on September 26, 1945, it was important to retrieve small missile parts to analyze success or failure. These searches routinely wasted countless man-hours as ground recovery crews scoured vast expanses of desert in search of often-buried missile fragments. That ended in 1961 with the introduction of the Missile Dogs: Dingo, a Weimaraner, and Count, a German Shorthair. For up to a year before firing, important components of a missile were sprayed with squalene, a shark-liver oil that the dogs could smell from hundreds of feet away. After a missile firing, Dingo and Count raced among the sands sniffing out the scent objects. With a 96% recovery rate, the program was so successful that other military and scientific agencies requested the services of the original Missile Dogs of White Sands. So yes, your dog is welcome anywhere in the world's largest gypsum sand dunes that form when minerals dissolve in nearby mountains during rainstorms.

And the Waggie for Best Canine Hike In Sand Dunes (Inland Division) goes to...

...White Sands National Park!

The dunes are not as imposing as others in the height game but instead of climbing just one or two your dog will have miles of bowls and dunes to play in across the white sands. There are even 6.2 miles of marked trails, including five on the *Alkili Flats Trail*. To follow along your dog can choose between maximum fun plowing up and down the dunes on the shortest route to the next post or save energy by navigating around the bowls. For what it is worth, the gypsum sands pack tighter than other dunes making it a less strenuous journey.

Since White Sands became a National Monument in 1933 dogs have been welcome anywhere in the dunes. The park moved up a pay grade to national park status in 2019 and hopefully nothing will change on that score.

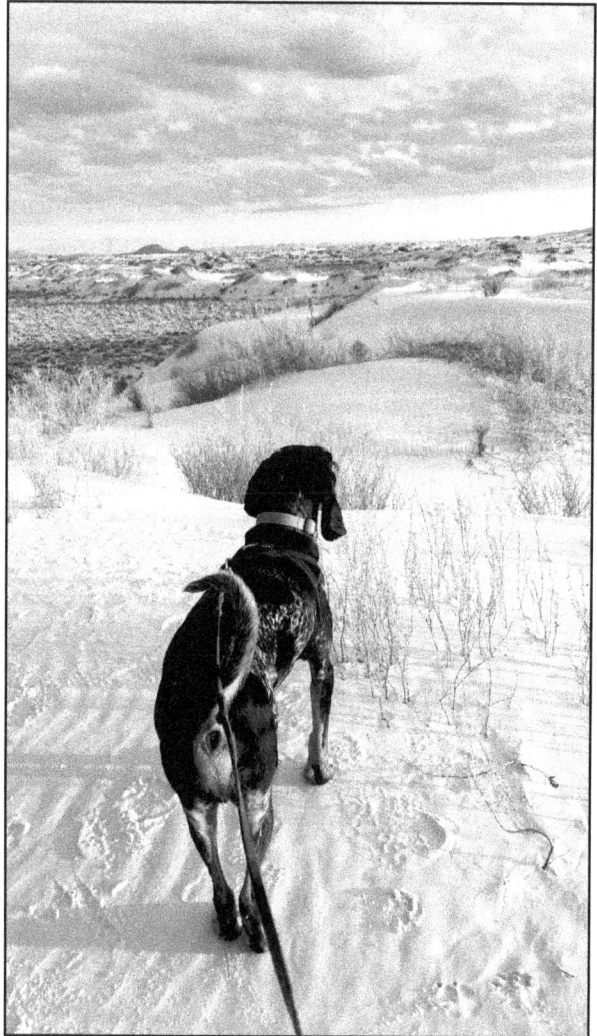

Best Canine Hike
Up an Iconic Mountain

Mountains hold a special place in the heart of canine hikers and America's iconic peaks fill bucket lists everywhere. Here are the nominees for the most best of the storied hikes with your dog to the top of a celebrated peak...

Adirondack Park - Mount Marcy (New York)
Van Hoevenberg Trail

Mount Marcy is the monarch of the 46 mountains that comprise the High Peaks of the Adirondacks, soaring 5,344 feet above sea level. A professor named Ebenezer Emmons led the first recorded ascent on August 5, 1837, naming the peak for New York Governor William Learned Marcy. Theodore Roosevelt was camping here when he learned he would become the nation's youngest president after William McKinley's assassination. Today Mount Marcy can be tagged on well-marked trails from four directions. The shortest route comes in from the north on the *Van Hoevenberg Trail*. It is still 7.4 miles one way, with an elevation gain of 3,224 feet. Despite those daunting numbers this hike is so popular you might think you are scaling a hill in a neighborhood park with your dog. Some claim it is the most visited "remote" peak in the United States.

Black Hills National Forest - Black Elk Peak (South Dakota)
Trail 9

The Lakota Sioux thought the craggy rock formations here resembled owls and worshiped the sacred site as Hirjhán Káǧa, or, "Owl Maker." The picture-postcard Sylvan Lake is a popular jumping off point to climb through Ponderosa pines, spruce, and aspen up Black Elk Peak, at 7,242 feet the highest point in America east of the Rocky Mountains. There is some rock scrambling near the top but your dog can make it all the way and even go up the steps into the abandoned stone fire tower. Views from the craggy open summit - the mountain has over 2,900 feet of prominence - reach into four states, including the world's largest buffalo herds that graze in Custer State Park.

Pike National Forest - Pikes Peak (Colorado)
Barr National Recreation Trail

Pikes Peak, with its prominence on the Front Range that made it the first landmark settlers saw heading West, is the most-visited mountain in the United States. Most drive or ride to the top but the 13-mile trek to the 14,110-foot summit built by Bill Barr in the 1910s is the choice of canine hikers. The journey gains nearly 8,000 feet in elevation - the biggest in Colorado - but is not overly steep however, with an average grade of 11%, and the *Barr Trail* is one of the Rocky Mountain State's most popular hikes. There are three miles of canine hiking above the treeline and no natural water sources so head out prepared.

Pisgah National Forest - Grandfather Mountain (North Carolina)
Daniel Boone Scout Trail

French botanist Andre Michaux excitedly scrawled in his journal in 1794, "Reached the summit of the highest mountain in all of North America!" Andre was wrong, of course, but he could be excused his enthusiasm as Grandfather Mountain, actually a collection of several peaks, rises so abruptly above its North Carolina surroundings. Calloway Peak, at 5,946 feet, is the highest spot to tag on the massif. For its abundance of rare and endangered plant species, Grandfather Mountain has been designated one of the world's few International Biosphere Reserves. There are 16 distinct ecosystems here and your dog will be hiking through most of them.

White Mountain National Forest - Mount Washington (New Hampshire)
Ammonoosuc Ravine Trail/Jewell Trail

You say you've always wanted to hike with your dog in the snow in July? It can happen at Mount Washington. The weather here is considered the worst in the world; winds have been recorded at 231 miles per hour and hurricane force gales over 75 mph blow one day in three. Dense fog visits the 6,288-foot summit 315 days a year. There are at least 15 long, rugged hiking trails up Mount Washington, the first of which was hacked out in 1819. Today it is the oldest continually used mountain trail in the United States. The *Ammonoosuc Ravine Trail* climbs up the western slopes, tracing the plunging Ammonoosuc River through the woods with stream crossings and waterfall views. If the weather is co-operating the *Jewell Trail*, that works along the cliffs with long exposed views, is a good option to come back down.

And the Waggie for Best Canine Hike Up an Iconic Mountain goes to...

...Black Hills National Forest!

What a tough category. I mean, wow. Maybe what puts the hike with your dog up Black Elk Peak - which was named Harney by American explorers in 1855 and has only recently honored its Lakota Sioux origins - over the top is Sylvan Lake with its calendar cover-worthy pool of water flanked by rounded granite boulders. Or it is *Trail 9* scenery - beguiling forests of spruce and Ponderosa pines and the sporty climb through crags at the top. Or it is the rich history - Crazy Horse cousin Black Elk received his "Great Vision" here when he was nine years old and General George Armstrong Custer's party are believed to be the first Americans to scale the summit on a gold-finding expedition. Or it is the views - both long and in the adjacent Black Hills are sublime. It all adds up to a tail-wagging winner for your dog on Black Elk Peak.

Best Canine Hike
To Bag a State Highpoint

Highpointing is the game of surmounting the highest point in any given geographic area and the division of America into states makes for a very attractive challenge. State highpointing is a wildly disparate pursuit - it could be walking across a parking lot in Delaware or donning full climbing gear to conquer the glacial Mount Rainier. With that in mind here are the nominees for best state highpoint to ascend to with your dog...

Black Mesa Nature Preserve - Black Mesa (Oklahoma)
Summit Trail

The "black" in the mesa in the far northwest tip of the Oklahoma Panhandle is a layer of lava rock that coated the region about 30 million years ago. The mesa is also the highest point in Oklahoma at 4,973 feet. The ascent to the roof of the Sooner State covers 4.2 miles and is dead flat the first half of the way before switchbacking up the rear of the mesa. There is nothing growing high enough to obscure the view of even a dachshund at any point on this canine hike.

Mount Greylock Reservation - Mount Greylock (Massachusetts)
Hopper/Mt. Prospect/Money Brook Trails

In 1844 Ralph Waldo Emerson urged his friend Henry David Thoreau to climb Mount Greylock, a place he described as "a serious mountain." More than 170 years later the climb up the highest point in southern New England (3,491 feet) is still the must-do major canine hike in the Berkshire Mountains. This 11-mile canine loop travels through some of the oldest trees in the Bay State and tags the summits of Mt. Prospect, Mt. Williams, and Greylock.

Mount Rogers National Recreation Area - Mount Rogers (Virginia)
Appalachian Trail

This is one highpoint adventure that gets it all backwards. The canine hike starts in wide open spaces with sweeping countryside vistas and ends up in a lush spruce forest where nothing can be seen but tree

trunks. Mount Rogers is the roof of the Commonwealth of Virginia and at 5,729 feet the loftiest state highpoint east of South Dakota that lacks a road to the summit. Getting there is one of the best Blue Ridge hikes with your dog on any of three routes. The most popular assault launches from Massie Gap; Mount Rogers is 4.5 miles away. Friendly horses could well tag along on the way through the meadows adding a dash of equine charm to this ramble.

San Isabel National Forest - Mount Elbert (North Carolina)
North Elbert Trail

The highest mountain in America's Lower 48 is California's Mount Whitney at 14,505 feet. You can hike with your dog to the shadow of the summit but the final steps will be yours alone as you leave dog-friendly Inyo National Forest and travel into Sequoia National Park, where dogs are banned from the trails. The highest spot in America where dogs are legally allowed to go is Mount Elbert in Colorado, only 65 feet lower than Whitney. No special gear required - your dog can hike all the way to the top. Just put one paw in front of the other.

Underhill State Park - Mount Mansfield (Vermont)
Sunset Ridge Trail

This canine hike starts out low voltage on an old gravel access road for one mile but your dog's ears will perk up when you break in the open and begin to enjoy nearly continuous ridgeline views. The destination is 4,393-foot Mount Mansfield and you will gain 2,568 feet to tag the roof of Vermont. The final two miles are across the largest patch of alpine tundra in the Green Mountain State. On a clear day at the summit the skyscrapers of Montreal are revealed in the 360-degree views.

And the Waggie for Best Canine Hike to Bag a State Highpoint goes to…

…San Isabel National Forest!

OK, maybe it's not a fair fight when Mount Elbert is more than twice as high as any of the other nominees…but c'mon, your dog can just walk there! It is so easy that snobbish alpinists once piled rocks on neighboring Mount Massive in an attempt to give it the extra twenty feet it would need to surpass Mount Elbert. Of course, "easy" is relative and all prudent precautions for being on a 14,440-foot mountain must be taken. But any trail dog accustomed to a ten-mile hike can scale Mount Elbert. There are five routes to the top, the most popular being the *North Elbert Trail*. From trailhead to summit is 4.5 miles, the first two climbing through alpine forests. After the trail bursts above the treeline the route switches back twice before pulling straight to the summit. No rock scrambling is even necessary. Views = amazing.

Best Canine Hike
to an Alpine Lake

The Big Three of Canine Hiking Destinations are Views, Waterfalls, and Lakes and the competition is certainly stiff in this important category with five unforgettable adventures as nominees...

Adirondack Park (New York)
Lake George

Canine hikers who complete the *Tongue Mountain Range Loop* above Lake George run out of superlatives to describe it. The journey begins in the middle of six summits on an isthmus that thrusts into the lake and crosses the three southern peaks - Fifth Peak, French Point Mountain, and First Peak - with memorable views of some of Lake George's 365 islands. Although these mountains never reach higher than 1,813 feet there are also several unnamed knobs that make the ascents and descents seem like your dog is climbing across the back of a stegosaurus. Your destination is the very Tip of the Tongue, where the mountain range plunges into Lake George. Here, wide rock perches make ideal diving boards for a well deserved jump in the lake for your dog.

Bridger-Teton National Forest (Wyoming)
Green River Lakes

The Wind River Range doesn't get as much hype as its famous neighbors at Yellowstone and the Tetons but there is more glacial activity here than any place in the Lower 48. That scouring and shaping has created the tallest mountain in the middle Rocky Mountains (Gannett Peak at 13,804 feet) and many spectacular alpine lakes. This canine hike on the *Highline Trail* actually starts at a lake - Lower Green Lake - but it goes to the even more impressive turquoise waters of Upper Green Lake.

Carson National Forest (New Mexico)
Williams Lake

At 11,040 feet in elevation Williams Lake is a proud member of the select club of two-mile high American lakes. The canine hike to the shallow waters kicks off in the Taos Ski Valley village and covers two miles. Although you gain about 1,000 feet in elevation the ramble through Engelmann spruce doesn't push straight up like many Rocky Mountain trails. Short, steep stretches intermingle with mostly level trail that recharges flagging dog's engines. The footpath swings into meadowland and scattered moraine fields from time to time as well. Williams Lake sits in a gorgeous natural bowl ringed by rocky peaks that are the handiwork of 10,000-year old glaciers. If everyone is feeling spry, it is two more miles to the roof of New Mexico atop one of those mountains, Wheeler Peak.

Grand Mesa National Forest (Colorado)
Eggleston Lake

You could just start at Eggleston Lake but then there would be no amazing hike for your dog on the *Crag Crest National Trail*. So kick off the 10.3-mile loop across the largest flat-topped mountain in the world at the western end and spend time in the wildflower-filled meadows and deep green Englemann spruce forests before tackling the craggy ridgeline and dropping down to the bracing waters of this alpine lake at 10,128 feet.

San Juan National Forest (Colorado)
Ice Lake

This is a tough go for any trail dog - straight uphill all the way. But this Waggie is for hikes to an alpine lake, right? And that lake is holding stunning blue waters nestled in a cirque of 13,700-foot mountains. The footpath begins at 9,840 feet and reaches Ice Lake at 12,260 feet in a little over three miles. Island Lake and Fuller Lake are a little further along. Old growth forest gives way to subalpine meadows that are choked with wildflowers beginning in mid-summer.

"I can't think of anything that brings me closer to tears than when my old dog
- completely exhausted after a hard day in the field -
limps away from her nice spot in front of the fire
and comes over to where I'm sitting and puts her head in my lap,
a paw over my knee, and closes her eyes, and goes back to sleep.
I don't know what I've done to deserve that kind of friend."
-Gene Hill

And the Waggie for Best Canine Hike to an Alpine Lake goes to...

...Bridger-Teton National Forest!

Talk about subjective - wake up tomorrow and the Waggie could easily go to any of the other nominees. The Green River Lakes get the nod with two widely contrasting hikes, the *Highline Trail* that rambles through an open meadow with constant views of the staggering Wind River Range and the *Lakeside Trail* that creates a loop with immersion into a dark spruce forest. The south shore features a broad pebble beach where your dog can swim beneath those jagged mountaintops. Pus further up the *Highline Trail* to Upper Green Lake and ever-closer views of Squaretop Mountain that has dominated this canine hike since the first steps. The turquoise waters lap up against the White Rock Cliffs and the trail visits more meadows beyond. Lastly, the Green River Lakes tickle the imagination. As the headwaters for the Green River, a primary feeder into the great Colorado River, the water where your dog is fetching will eventually flow through the Grand Canyon.

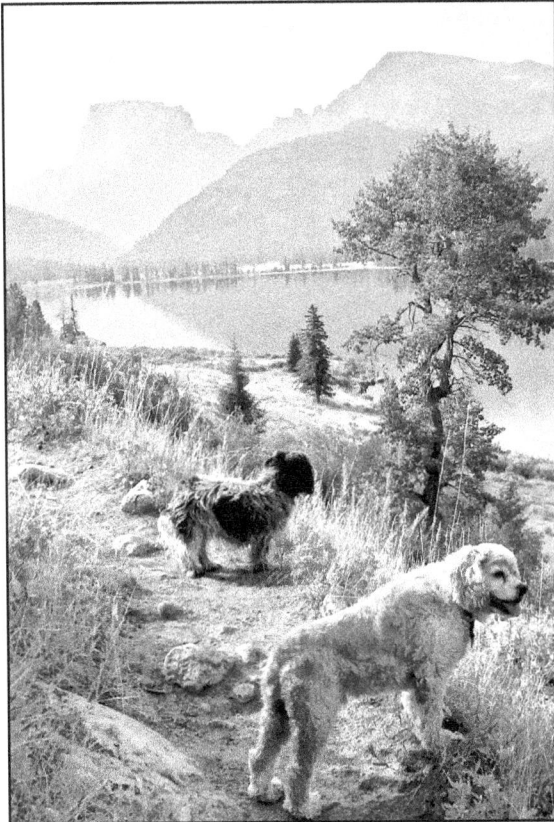

Best Canine Hike
to a Waterfall (Northeast Division)

Waterfalls are like jerky treats to trail dogs, plenty of canine hikes have launched with a hyrdospectacular as its destination. Too many to be contained in a single category so the Waggies have to be split up geographically...

Catskill Forest Preserve (New York)
Kaaterskill Falls

Niagara Falls is not the highest waterfall in New York State and for a good part of the 19th century it wasn't even the most famous. Kaaterskill Falls, a two-tiered water plunge with a slight lefthand turn in the Hudson Valley, is that destination. The upper ribbon of water drops a full 175 feet - the same as Niagara Falls - and the lower falls tumble another 75 feet into a rocky basin. Recent trail improvements bring new options to viewing one of America's oldest tourist attractions on Spruce Creek.

Fillmore Glen State Park (New York)
Cowsheds

The main canine hiking experience at Fillmore Glen is on the *Gorge Trail* that crosses Dry Creek on nine bridges and visits five major waterfalls. Much of the sublime stonework along the trail was constructed by Civilian Conservation Corps stonemasons during the Great Depression. This is an easy trot for your dog for two miles into the glen, starting flat and becoming increasingly steep as you reach the end of the gorge. Opportunities for doggie dips abound but none so picturesque as the natural swimming pool beyond the Cowsheds, a magazine cover-worthy waterfall that drops into a semi-circular amphitheater.

Letchworth State Park (New York)
Middle Falls

When William Letchworth donated his 1,000-acre Glen Iris estate along the Genessee River to New York it quickly become one of the corner stones of the Empire State park system. Dubbed the "Grand Canyon of the East," the wooded gorge was scraped and shaped by glaciers, leaving some of the country's most dramatic waterfalls in their wake. The *Gorge Trail* traces the ravine for seven miles and visits three major hydrospectaculars in the first two. All the Genessee River falls are Niagara-wide; the Middle Falls oozes the most personality and is the highest of the trio at 107 feet.

Ricketts Glen State Park (Pennsylvania)
Kitchen Creek

A good waterfall trail might yield three, maybe four waterfalls. How about a trail that goes past 23 named waterfalls? That's what you find with your dog find on a hike on the magical *Falls Trail*, a Y-shaped exploration along two branches of Kitchen Creek. 19th century timber baron and Civil War hero R. Bruce Ricketts hired a crew to build a trail along and across the plunging waters and the project took 28 years. One of the most uniquely scenic areas in the Northeast, Ricketts Glen was slated to become a national park in the 1930s but World War II shelved plans for this development. Instead, the Glens Natural Area trundles on as a National Natural Landmark.

Swallow Falls State Park (Maryland)
Muddy Creek Falls

The *Falls Trail* navigates through a grove of white pines and hemlocks that are the oldest trees in Maryland, estimated to have been flourishing for almost 400 years. Philanthropist Henry Krug refused to allow the trees to be harvested in the gorge and when a World War I plan to dam the Youghiogheny River fell through their survival was assured. The destination for your dog is Muddy Creek Falls, the Free State's highest single water drop at 53 feet. Although your best trail companion won't get overheated under the cool, dark hemlocks there are so many enticing doggie swimming holes on the one-mile loop you may want to block off an entire afternoon for your visit.

And the Waggie for Best Canine Hike to a Waterfall (Northeast Division) goes to...

...Ricketts Glen State Park!

There is a Hollywood story, NSFW, about Milton Berle that informs the awarding of the Waggie to Ricketts Glen. The prettiest falls in all of the Glens Natural Area may be where the Kitchen Creek descends into a copse of towering hemlocks and oaks before tumbling over three cascades. And Adams Falls is across the street from the *Falls Trail* and not even included in the roster of 23 named falls. Kitchen Creek slices through the Ganoga Glen to the left (the tallest water display, 94-foot Ganoga Falls is here) and Glen Leigh to the right before uniting at Waters Meet. The two prongs of the trail connect at the top of the twin falls via the 1.2-mile *Highland Trail*. The complete falls experience encompasses almost seven miles. Today the 130-year old *Falls Trail* remains a maintenance challenge and its steep grades can be muddy and slippery so your dog's four-wheel traction will be most welcome.

"Any man who does not like dogs and want them does not deserve to be in the White House."
-Calvin Coolidge

Best Canine Hike
to a Waterfall (Southeast Division)

The waterfalls of the Southeast are legendary with streams plunging off the ancient Appalachian Mountains in such an abundance it would require a lifetime of canine hiking to inventory them all. The nominees for the Waggie stress their uniqueness among the water display community...

Amicalola Falls State Park (Georgia)
Amicalola Falls

The Cherokee named this 729-foot high cascade Amicalola which translates to "tumbling waters." The falls are the centerpiece of one of Georgia's most popular parks - and the park service has given your dog a cornucopia of ways to experience the plunging water. A conventional dirt trail ascends Little Amicalola Creek, that is one option. Or ascend a 600-step staircase that works its way up the face of the famous falls, eventually crossing in front of the main drop. When you get back down you can hike with your dog on an 8.5-mile approach trail to the southern terminus of the *Appalachian Trail*.

Cumberland Falls State Park (Tennessee)
Cumberland Falls

The largest falls on the Cumberland River - 65 feet high and 125 feet wide - likes to bill itself as the "Niagara of the South." The hydrospectacular is a far sight short of that but Cumberland has something Niagara, or any falls in the Western Hemisphere, does not have: a moonbow. Adventurous dog owners will want to sneak off to the other side of the river from the observation platforms where *Trail 9* offers some of the best peeks of Cumberland Falls. At 1.5 miles, this natural surface trail seems benign enough but if you complete all of *Trail 9* your dog will know they have had a workout. At river level Eagle Falls, a worthy water spout in its own right, serves up a plunge pool for canine aquatics before heading back up.

DuPont State Forest (North Carolina)
Wintergreen Falls

The marquee water displays in the state forest are the photo-hungry triad of Hooker Falls, Triple Falls, and High Falls which are connected by a single trail. But the nominee for the Waggie will look to a supporting star, the much-less visited Wintergreen Falls, tucked into a gorgeous setting where the 20-foot water spout makes a 90-degree left turn through the rocky terrain. There are several tree-shrouded routes - 90 named trails explore DuPont State Forest - to the falls but the shortest requires a three-mile round trip for your dog.

Falling Waters State Park (Florida)
Falling Waters

The highest elevation in the Sunshine State is only 345 feet yet the Falling Waters drop an impressive 73 feet. How? The trick is that most of the water falls underground into a sinkhole. At Falling Waters State Park you take your dog into woods of towering Southern pines and Northern hardwoods but it doesn't take long for this hike to cease to resemble a typical forest walk. In short order you are introduced to fern-draped sinkholes, the namesake waterfall, a wiregrass prairie, and a two-acre lake. Your dog will be trotting on elaborate boardwalks and the remnants of old country roads throughout the park to experience Branch Creek disappearing underground.

William B. Bankhead National Forest (Alabama)
Fall Creek Falls

With nearly 25,000 acres under protection, Sipsey Wilderness is the third largest wilderness area in the country east of the Mississippi River. Wild-flowing creeks in northwestern Alabama gang up to become the Sipsey River, 61 miles of which has been designated Wild and Scenic. Enough water tumbles over cracks in limestone foundations that Sipsey has been hailed as the "Land of 1,000 Waterfalls." Many of the waterfalls can't be reached by trail regardless - when you hear falling water start bushwhacking through the forest to find the source, often drips over wide, moss-covered rock ledges. Fall Creek Falls reigns as the monarch of Sipsey water displays.

And the Waggie for Best Canine Hike to a Waterfall (Southeast Division) goes to...

...William B. Bankhead National Forest!

The Waggie goes to the Sipsey Wilderness, a land of waterfalls, sinkholes, and sandstone bluffs that is a popular backpacking destination for planting yourself in a camp and exploring the marvelously lubricated second-growth forest. Of the official trails, canine day hikers favor *Trail 209* that links several of the established dirt passages through the unmarked wilderness. Fall Creek Falls, a 90-foot water spout near the convergence of the Sipsey River and Fall Creek splashes onto a jumble of boulders directly on the trail.

Traveling south from the Borden Creek Bridge trailhead the journey is less than three miles; this is as lovely a hike as you can take with your dog to a waterfall but involves a water crossing on a sandy creek bed and a memorable 100-foot passage through a narrow rock cave. Allow plenty of time for the journey as it will be a chore to keep urging your water-loving dog away from the many swimming diversions along the way.

Best Canine Hike
to a Waterfall (Midwest Division)

The glacially carved topography of the Midwest more than makes up for the lack in elevation so there are no shortage of quality nominees for Best Canine Hike to a Waterfall...

Gooseberry Falls State Park (Minnesota)
Fifth Falls

The westernmost edge of Lake Superior is characterized by craggy headlands blanketed in thick coatings of pine and birch. Along the coast dozens of fast-flowing streams are showcased cascading down small mountains to mingle with the waters of the Great Lakes. Five of those hard-charging water spouts surge down the Gooseberry River on Minnesota's North Shore. The Upper, Middle, and Lower Falls hog most of the visitors with easy access on stairways and boardwalks so canine hikers will want to aim inland for Fifth Falls. This ramble is never taxing for your dog and there are calm spots in the energetic river to host a doggie dip.

Hocking Hills State Park (Ohio)
Cedar Falls

The last Ice Age may have done its best work in this valley the tribes of the Wyandot, Delaware and Shawnee knew as "Hockhocking" for its bottle shape. Hocking Hills State Park is a superb destination for any dog, but is especially delightful for the canine hiker who is a few hikes beyond those days of the 10-mile treks. There are six destination areas in the park - five open for canine exploring - that visit a collection of seven waterfalls. Big Spring Hollow Falls is the highest with a drop of over 100 feet but Cedar Falls disgorges the greatest volume of water that collects into a perfect doggie swimming pool.

Roughlock Falls Nature Area (South Dakota)
Roughlock Falls

Scientists estimate Spearfish Canyon is six times as old as the Grand Canyon. The 400-foot high limestone cliffs lord over some of the greatest botanical diversity in the Black Hills. The multi-channeled waters of Roughlock Falls pour down from Little Spearfish Creek just before entering Spearfish Canyon. The enchanting water display is reached via an easy ramble through Spearfish Canyon with an elevation gain of about 150 feet or via a wooden bridge system from the Falls Nature Area. This nominated canine hike is a jumble of tumbling waters, pools reflecting mossy boulders, and towering Ponderosa pines.

Tahquamenon Falls State Park (Michigan)
Tahquamenon Waters

Only two waterfalls east of the Mississippi River send more water over their lip than the Upper Tahquamenon Falls. The Upper is only 50 feet high but a massive 200 feet across, creating a supreme curtain of water. That water is a sparkling golden brown thanks to tree tannins leeched into the river from cedar swamps upstream. There is also a Lower Falls, a series of five cascades and tumbles around an island in the Tahquamenon River that sketches a wide panorama. A 4.8-mile trail connects the two. The dirt path is a narrow and rooty affair with plenty of ups and downs to pique your dog's interest. The spruce and cedar and hemlock shroud this entire canine hike but views of the close-by river come at regular intervals.

Tettegouche State Park (Minnesota)
High Falls

The Baptism River has been working on the rugged rhyolite ridges above the Lake Superior shoreline for one billion years. There is still plenty of work to be done as witnessed by the highest waterfall wholly contained in the state of Minnesota (Canada claims half the droplets from the higher Pigeon River High Falls that helps form the international border). The *High Falls Trail* is a broad brown brush stroke of dirt through a lush North Woods forest of birch, aspen, and pine. This is a 1.5-mile one-way canine hike to reach the 70-foot High Falls but there are side delights along the way, including multiple viewpoints of the vivacious Baptism River. A ten-minute side trail leads to a wide double drop in the river known as Two Step Falls. The trail continues down a long set of wooden steps to a swinging suspension bridge at water level leading your water-loving dog to the plunge pool.

And the Waggie for Best Canine Hike to a Waterfall (Midwest Division) goes to...

...Hocking Hills State Park!

The star of Hocking Hills is Old Man's Cave tucked into a heavily wooded, twisting ravine. The Old Man was Richard Rowe who moved to the area some time around 1796 to establish a trading post. Upon arriving in Hocking Hills he stayed and lived out his life here, traveling with his two dogs in search of game. Rowe is buried beneath the ledge of the main recess cave. An easy, one-mile trail works its way into and around the primeval gorge; wooden steps and bridges smooth the way. No word about the dogs. The two main natural attractions that Old Man Rowe would have known intimately are Ash Cave, with its waterfall behind which he could walk his dogs, and the twisting Cedar Falls where his buddies no doubt swam. A rollicking six-mile trail worthy of a Waggie connects it all.

Best Canine Hike to a Waterfall (Western Division)

The West is where the big boys of American waterfalls, heightwise, reside. Many are contained in national parks, sequestered away from curious canine eyes. Don't despair, we've rounded up some stellar nominees for best hike with your dog to a waterfall in the West...

Columbia River Gorge National Scenic Area (Oregon)
Multnomah Falls

Created by a cataclysmic blast of glacial lake water 15,000 years ago, the Columbia River flows through one of the few east-west canyons in the world. Some 77 waterfalls tumble off ridges and sheer walls that soar 2,000 feet above the river. Included in this hydrospectacular bounty is the largest concentration of high waterfalls in North America. No wonder the Columbia River Gorge between Oregon and Washington was designated America's first National Scenic Area. Multnomah Falls is the emperor of Columbia Gorge waterfalls with a year-round plunge of 620 feet in two sheer drops.

Custer Gallatin National Forest (Montana)
Grotto Falls

South of Bozeman, Custer Gallatin National Forest bursts with 2,000 miles of trails and the canine hike along Hyalite Creek through a U-shaped glaciated canyon encapsulates the beauty of them all. There are three primo destinations in Hyalite Canyon, depending on your trail dog's hunger for adventure. Grotto Falls is the most popular of the many side spurs that lead to waterfalls spilling into the canyon. Inclines are easy and the coniferous forest thick as the trail makes several crossings of Hyalite Creek. In a little over two miles the wide and frothy waters plunge into an inviting doggie swimming hole.

Gifford Pinchot National Forest (Washington)
Falls Creek Falls

Tucked deep into the Gifford Pinchot National Forest, Falls Creek charges down basaltic cliffs in three tiers, with the lower two being most on display. The middle tier spreads out in a 90-foot veil before collecting itself in a final 70-foot cataract that powers into the rock bowl at the bottom. Additional trails bring access to the 60-foot top of the hydrospectacular. A full exploration for your dog will cover over six miles and include mossy rocks, bracing pools for canine dips, and a swinging wooden suspension bridge.

Lake Tahoe Basin Management Unit (California)
Cascade Falls/Eagle Falls Trail

With all the mind-bending views available of Lake Tahoe it is saying something when the overlook of Emerald Bay at Inspiration Point claims to be the most photographed spot in America. Most people just park and point their smartphones but your dog can do better at one of the world's largest alpine lakes. Across the street from Inspiration Point is a one-mile trip to Cascade Falls that gains scarcely 100 feet in elevation on the trip. This is absolutely wonderful canine hiking terrain with widely dispersed Jeffrey pines and rocks that appear to have been interjected for decoration rather than obstacles. You never actually get a full-on look at the 200-foot falls but the final steps across open granite slopes will bring your dog to the side of the water display which can be powerfully impressive during late spring snow melts.

Whiskeytown National Recreation Area (California)
Whiskeytown Falls

How does a 220-foot waterfall remain unknown in America's most populous state until 2004? The Whiskeytown community digs its roots out of the California Gold Rush. The town supposedly got its name when a mishap-prone miner named Billie Peterson lost a whiskey barrel while hauling supplies. The keg tumbled down the hillside and broke on the rocks, spilling into what became known as Whiskey Creek. Miners knew of the jaw-dropping falls and so did loggers but no one spread the word. After these 42,000 acres became federal property in the 1960s there were no funds to protect the natural treasure. It was left off maps and eventually forgotten. It wasn't until an aerial survey rediscovered the three-tier plunge. Now there is a 1.7-mile trail to Whiskeytown Falls, hard-packed and wide enough - barely - for old log trucks, in the beginning before climbing... and climbing...and climbing. There aren't many downhill pawfalls before reaching the Wintu View overlook.

And the Waggie for Best Canine Hike to a Waterfall (Western Division) goes to...

...Columbia River Gorge National Scenic Area!

This is the biggest natural attraction in the Pacific Northwest with two million visitors stopping each year. Most won't venture past the overlook at Multnomah Falls Lodge. Many will go to the historic Benson Bridge across the middle and some will even follow the switchbacking paved path for 1.2 miles to the very top of the iconic cataract but few will continue on to see why Multnomah Falls takes home the Waggie.

Steering your dog onto the *Larch Mountain Trail* (#441) into the lush old growth forest brings more waterfalls. In less than one mile, link into the *Wahkeena Trail* (#420) for the walk back down. Fairy Falls, a lovely fan-style waterfall, highlights this leg of the canine hike. Near the bottom of the 4.8-mile loop the natural surface trail passes hard by the 242-foot Wahkeena Falls that squeezes through a moss-covered volcanic cliff. That will give your dog over 1,000 feet of waterfalls for only a few hours purchase.

Best Canine Hike
to a Waterfall (Desert Southwest Division)

Waterfalls are always captivating but nowhere more so than in the desert; the nominees for sniffing out the best hike with your dog to an unexpected oasis are...

Cococino National Forest (Arizona)
Fossil Creek Falls

The rough and rocky 21-mile access road is the only tough part of this canine hike. To reach the falls flowing over a 25-foot cliff requires a one mile hike tracing the crystal clear waters of Fossil Creek as they mingle with the desert landscape. The plunge pool is big and deep enough to encourage divers to leap off the cliff. The fact that anyone bothers to go to Fossil Creek Falls at all given the entrance road proves why this canine hike merits a nomination for a Waggie.

Coronado National Forest (Arizona)
Tanque Verde Falls

If there's water in the wash when you start out you can be sure your hike will conclude with the stars of this nominated hike - a 30-foot water spout and another plunge of the Tanque Verde River of 80 feet. Don't let the early easy descent into the canyon fool you; when it is time to head upstream there will be rock scrambling for your dog and wet paws needed to negotiate the route to the falls, about two miles away.

Grand Staircase-Escalante National Monument (Utah)
Lower Calf Creek Falls

What is the perfect end to a hike with your dog? An unforgettable photo-op for you and a refreshing swim for him? If that's your definition of the ideal adventure denouement pull off of Scenic Byway Route 12 and jump on the trail to Lower Calf Creek Falls. After three miles the trail halts at the foot of a desert dreamscape that could have come straight from a Hollywood western. A crystal clear perennial stream spills 126 feet down the mineral-streaked cliff walls. While you fumble with your iPhone for the perfect photo angle your dog will sprint into the generous plunge pool for a well-deserved swim.

Red Cliffs Recreation Area (Utah)
Red Reef Falls

Summer may dry up the Quail Creek waterfalls in Red Reef Canyon and all your dog will be left with here is a fun little hike. Other times the *Red Reef Trail* works its way up a sculpted, intimate canyon populated by small waterfalls and pools. The official trail ends where Red Reef Falls fills nearly the width of the canyon narrows. Your trail dog may point out the moki steps carved into the soft sandstone rock on the right side of the waterfall. Climb up and over and your and your adventure in the Red Cliffs can continue for miles more.

Tonto National Forest (Arizona)
Water Wheel Falls

Your trail dog will be having so much fun on this little hike they won't even notice how easy going it is along the East Verde Falls. Water Wheel Falls twists through the rocks into a broad swimming hole that could occupy fetching dogs for hours. Keeping on past the falls, however, the confluence with Ellison Creek brings with more cascades and more swimming holes.

And the Waggie for Best Canine Hike to a Waterfall (Desert Southwest Division) goes to…

…Grand Staircase-Escalante National Monument!

The Taylor Swift…*The Titanic*…the Hamilton…of the Waggie Awards - the Lower Calf Creek Falls. The reward for a classic desert canine hike of desert-varnished Navajo sandstone cliffs, canyon-shrouded gambrel oaks and boxelder, thickets of Mormon tea, and a crystal clear perennial stream is a stunning 126-foot water drop that hugs the open rock face. The waters gather in a doggie swimming pool for the ages before continuing down the canyon. The footpath is sandy under paw and the going can be slow, which fits this winning canine hike perfectly. The mostly level track climbs into the rocks for a spell, working around the marshy areas of Calf Creek.

Lower Calf Creek Falls can be your perfect ending - or not; there is also an Upper Calf Creek Falls, an 88-foot cataract with its own doggie swimming hole that is reached with a short, strenuous hike from Scenic Byway Route 12.

Best Canine Hike along a Riverside

Sometimes a great hike with your dog can be along an easy-flowing river where the languid waters infuse the mood of the outing. The waters never get too energetic and time seems to slip away. The nominees for the best day with your dog on a riverside are...

Flaming Gorge National Recreation Area (Utah)
Green River

Trailblazing 19th century scientist and explorer John Wesley Powell named the Flaming Gorge after he saw the sun shining off the red canyon walls on his epic 1869 exploration of the Green and Colorado rivers. Powell would recognize those walls today but the 502-foot high dam built in 1962 has changed the appearance of the Green River forever. Your dog might even spot a few plump trout in the crystalline waters that are the quarry of anglers floating merrily along - 22-pounders have been pulled from this stretch of the Green River.

Hillsborough River State Park (Florida)
Hillsborough River

The jungle-like woodlands that envelop the Hillsborough River include the requisite Florida sabal palms, cypress-filled wetlands and groves of wild citrus trees. Just the tiniest bit of elevation brings stands of hickory and sweetgum. On the bluffs above the river are amazing ancient live oaks. It is little wonder this slice of "wild Florida" was one of the nine original state parks created in the 1930s. The *Seminole Trail* loop visits them all, spending half of its 3.4 miles hard by the river and half inland. Since the canine hiking is on the north side of the Hillsborough River and the main park is on the south side a swinging wooden suspension bridge gets your dog underway.

Mount Hood National Forest (Oregon)
Salmon River

Sometimes you just want to take an easy, scenic hike with your dog. Welcome to the *Old Salmon River Trail*. Most of the magnificent old growth forests of the Pacific Northwest are not easy for canine hikers to get to - their inaccessibility is why they were never logged in the first place. Somehow the giant trees along the Salmon River survived, even after a paved road was built into the area. All the more remarkable when a single 10-foot thick Western red cedar tree can yield $10,000 worth of lumber. This quintessential Oregon canine hike is almost completely level on a generous needle-infused path. The Salmon River is your constant companion and side trails scoot down to pockets of sandy beach and deep pools perfect for doggie dips.

Sacramento River Trail (California)
Sacramento River

Redding, which began life in 1872 as a temporary supply center for the California & Oregon Railroad and is named for the line's railroad agent, fancies itself as one of the country's trail meccas. It is not false bravado - there are 225 miles of trails within 15 miles of town and the National Trails Association keeps its headquarters here. To find the crown jewel of the City of Redding trail system go no further than the town center. The *Sacramento River National Recreation Trail* winds easily along both sides of California's longest river on a flat, 12-foot wide paved surface that covers 11 miles in total, with many options to shorten your dog's hiking day. The views are splendid, the weather almost always sunny, and the trotting easy but the lasting thrills of the *Sacramento River Trail* are its award-winning bridges.

Wharton State Forest (New Jersey)
Batsto River

The New Jersey Pine Barrens are a tapestry of impenetrable scrub forest, cedar swamps, and peat bogs. The land is so mysterious it is the home of the legendary winged creature with the head of a horse supported by a four-foot serpentine body known as the "Jersey Devil." The Pine Barrens are lubricated by the slow-moving Batsto River, stained the color of tea by cedar sap, adding to the region's mystique. One million acres of undeveloped land reside in the heart of America's most densely populated state here, including the bulk of Philadelphia financier Joseph Wharton's former 100,000-acre estate. The *Batona Trail* slices 50.2 miles through this unworldly wilderness, marked by its distinctive pink blazes. This is easy walking on paw-friendly sand for most of its length, especially when it meets up with the mysterious Batsto.

And the Waggie for Best Canine Hike along a Riverside goes to...

...Flaming Gorge Recreation Area!

The delights of the *Little Hole National Recreation Trail*, a one-way walk below the Flaming Gorge Dam, clinch the Waggie. The river is constrained by red shale and sandstone cliffs while the level, easy-going footpath hugs the water's edge for most of its first couple of miles before ascending gradually 1,000 feet above the water. Short boardwalks conquer tricky areas in the canyon. You can turn back any time on this out-and-back ramble but the further you go the further you will want to go. Of course, your paddle-loving dog is likely to spend as much time in the crystal green waters as on the trail.

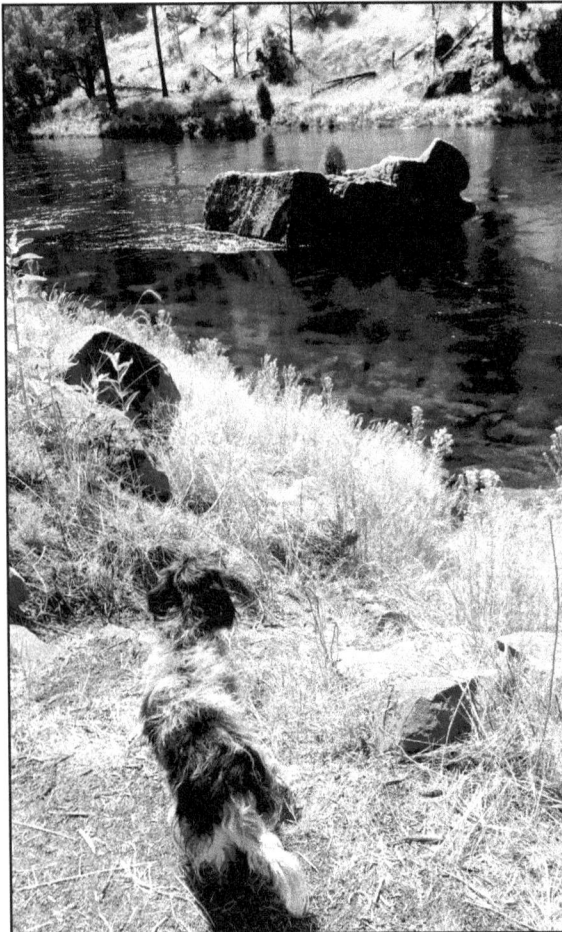

The Green River eventually emerges from Red Canyon and spreads out at the Little Hole Recreation Area after six miles. The parking area here makes this a candidate for a vehicle shuttle canine hike as well.

Best Canine Hike to a Doggie Swimming Hole

There is no point in having a favorite doggie swimming hole if every dog knows about it so the Waggie for Best Doggie Swimming Hole will remain a secret. But there are five nominees waiting for your dog to dive into that are up for the "almost best" doggie swimming hole...

Gunpowder Falls State Park (Maryland)
Sweathouse Trail

In the Belair section of this sprawling park in northeast Maryland the trail spends hours along the Gunpowder River until the last rapids are exhausted. But it is a feeder stream, Long Green Run, that hides the best doggie swimming hole in the Free State. Racing water is funneled into a deep pool by a whale-shaped rock that works as a natural diving board for playful dogs.

Jefferson National Forest (Virginia)
Devil's Fork Loop Trail

The full loop covers seven miles but this is one canine hike that plays better as an out-and-back. The star attraction is the Devil's Bathtub 1.6 miles from the trailhead. Getting there will take your dog into the cold Devil's Fork waters 12 times - and that won't even be their favorite part of the hike. And it is not even the Devil's Bathtub. It is the remarkably blue-green swimming hole that many people mistake for the tub (that is actually about 500 feet further on and up) that your dog will find irresistible.

Mark Twain National Forest (Missouri)
Blue Spring Trail

The *Blue Spring Trail* passes by easily under ledges of cherty Gasconite dolomite that spice up the canine hike. At this point you are hard by the North Fork River which is muddy and brown and giving up no hints of the wonders it holds up ahead. In less than one mile the star of the hike emerges, the natural spring nestled in a dramatic rock amphitheater, disgorging seven million gallons of water per day. If you didn't know better you would think this large grotto with turquoise blue water was designed specifically as a doggie swimming hole. Rock blocks line the edges for dogs to plunge into the pool and there is also a level bank for walking easily into the constant 57-degree water.

Nantahala National Forest (North Carolina)
Little Green Trail #485

There are eight significant waterfalls in the Panthertown Valley, a unique flat-bottomed valley in the Blue Ridge Mountains, and the grand tour takes in five in a roughly nine-mile loop. The bottomlands are lubricated by clear bronze streams with many opportunities for dog paddling. The first big chance comes at Schooltown Falls where it will take some considerable coaxing to get your water-loving dog away from the plunge pool and large fluffy sand beach to continue the hike.

Uinta-Wasatch-Cache National Forest (Utah)
Dog Lake Trail

Dog Lake is certainly no secret swimming hole. In fact, if there are no dogs paddling and fetching in the small mountain cirque when you arrive look around suspiciously. Shaded by trees, the dirt path switchbacks languidly to tame the 1,200 feet in elevation gain through Millcreek Canyon over three miles. Your dog can walk straight into the puddle-like lake from anywhere around its entire circumference and, if your arm is strong enough, swim for a stick from one shore to the other. Dogs are welcome at Dog Lake any day of the week but on odd number dates can romp on this trail off-lead.

"To err is human, to forgive, canine."
-Anonymous

And the Waggie for Best Canine Hike to a Swimming Hole goes to…

…Nantahala National Forest!

The Forest Service tried to keep the Panthertown Valley a secret as long as possible, only recently creating an "official" trail system blazed by volunteers enamored by the magic this place works on the hiking soul. A Panthertown tour of doggie swimming holes spends long level stretches on sandy dirt that is easy on the paw. A particularly delightful patch is along the Great Wall Trail through light woods paralleling a 300-foot high granite rock dome that has caused some to call this - unironically - the "Yosemite of the East." The canine hiking becomes more challenging at this point and a side trip to the top of the 4,206-foot Big Green Mountain is possible for views across Panthertown. Oh, the big cats are gone from Panthertown but this is a protected sanctuary for American black bears.

Best Canine Day Hike
on the Appalachian Trail

The idea for a footpath up the spine of the Appalachian Mountains was hatched by Benton MacKaye, a forester, in 1921. MacKaye wanted to provide an epic trail that would link farms and wilderness camps for the benefit of city-dwellers. Construction began in New York in 1923 and today the *Appalachian Trail* runs through 14 states for more than 2,100 miles after leaving Springer Mountain in Georgia. The trail is within a day's drive of 200 million people. Only a few of those 200 million will embark on a thru-hike but there are plenty of opportunities for a thrilling canine day hike and here are the nominees for the best...

Bear Mountain/Harriman State Park (New York)

When it was time to start building the *Appalachian Trail*, this is where they began. The Timp Hike starts directly on Route 9W with an un-promising break in the roadside weeds but spirits pick up once the remnants of the Dunderberg Spiral Railway, an incline railroad planned in 1890 but never finished, are reached. There are tunnels and an old railbed that serves as part of the trail. Heading up the *Ramapo-Dunderberg Trail*, the views of the Hudson River arrive and you realize why tons of money was burned trying to build a tourist railway here. The route rolls up and down mountains through boulder foundations until your dog covers the Timp, a peak overlooking the interior of the Hudson Highlands.

Cherokee National Forest (Tennessee)

The parking lot in Culver Gap is at the center of the five peaks that make up Roan Mountain, the only time the *Appalachian Trail* rises above 6,000 feet. Hiking north, after a very short stay in a spruce-fir forest your dog will be enjoying stunning unobstructed 360-degree views for seven miles across the summits of three grassy balds where trees refuse to root. It the longest such stretch in the Appalachian Mountains. A full day of splendid canine hiking can be carved out here but save time for the south side as well.

Delaware Water Gap National Recreation Area (New Jersey)

Here the *Appalachian Trail* skips along the Kittatinny Ridge where a detour passes Sunfish Pond, one of the Garden State's "7 Natural Wonders," where the water in the glacial lake is so clear and deep for a long time it was considered to be bottomless. The twisting *Red Dot Trail* up 1,527-foot Mount Tammany creates a loop with the white-blazed *Appalachian Trail*. It requires 1.5 miles of climbing on the rocky slopes to ascend the 1,200 feet to the top of the Delaware Water Gap that delivered the most famous 19th century views in America.

Pennsylvania State Game Lands #110 (Pennsylvania)

Thru-hikers on the *Appalachian Trail* like to say that Pennsylvania is where boots go to die. Rocks are certainly a theme on this canine hike from extended boulder hopping to the jumble of rock ledges that deliver the finest panoramas in the Keystone State. The two stars are Pulpit Rock and The Pinnacle. Pulpit Rock overlooks a river of quartzite boulders 500 feet wide and a half-mile long known as the Blue Rocks, souvenirs of the last ice age. A giant rock cairn signals the turnoff to the many rock ledge overlooks at the Pinnacle for your dog to gaze at the cultivated fields of the Cumberland Valley stretching to the horizon below. Here, the *Appalachian Trail* links with a fire road to create a nine-mile loop to the ridges along Blue Mountain.

White Mountain National Forest (New Hampshire)

Sooner or later all trail dogs make their way to Franconia Notch in the White Mountains, the only day hike in the Lower 48 on National Geographic's list of the "World's Best Hikes: 20 Dream Trails." The ascent to Franconia Ridge is accomplished on the grueling "45," climbing 3,840 feet in only four miles. Awaiting atop the ridge is the *Appalachian Trail* and the fabled knife-edge - exposed rock that dips and rolls for 1.7 thrilling miles. If you catch a clear day the views, including the entire Presidential Range, are the best in New England. The leg back down is on the *Old Bridle Path* that will give a new appreciation of the sturdiness of horses before the coming of the automobile. When the long, rocky descent across open slopes dips into stunted pines the nine-mile loop is coming to its rewarding end.

And the Waggie for Best Canine Day Hike on the Appalachian Trail goes to...

...Cherokee National Forest!

Breaking the tie of spectacular views with the other nominees is the largest rhododendron garden in the world. When the blooms stage one of the country's finest coming-out parties in June, tour buses make their way up Roan Mountain into Tollhouse Gap. It lends credence to Native American lore that a great battle between the Cherokees and Catawbas left the rhododendron stained crimson and the mountain treeless. The lush, mossy trail leads to the highest backcountry shelter on the entire 2,174-mile *Appalachian Trail*. Save for some short patches of rock-stepping the million dollar views from the only trail stretches over 6,000 feet are obtained with little purchase on Round Bald, Jane Bald, and at 6,189 feet, Grassy Ridge Bald. Roan Mountain is the kind of place you can imagine having a booming Kodak concession in the parking lot in the days before digital photography.

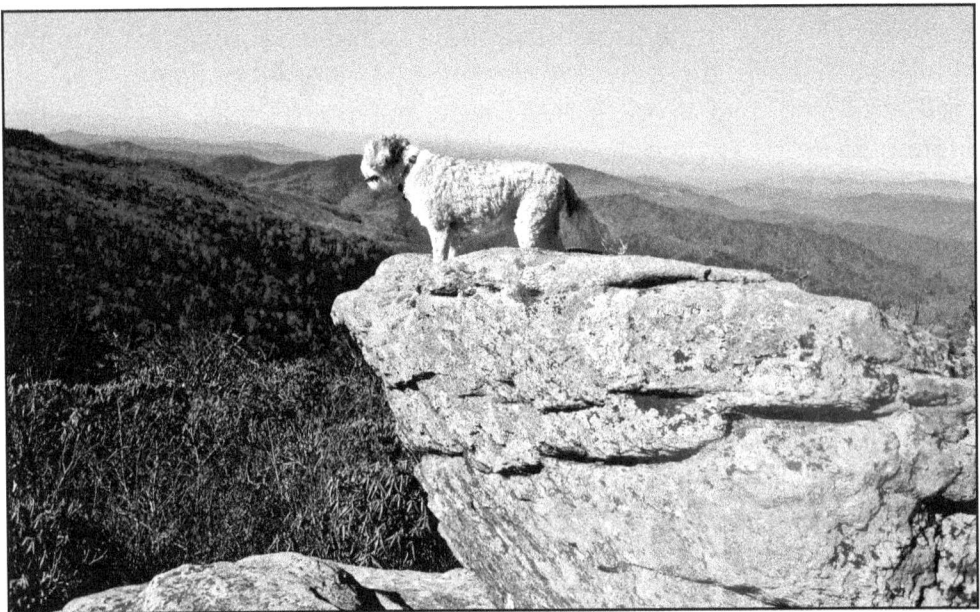

Best Canine Hike
on the Blue Ridge Parkway

Begun as a Depression-era public works project, the Blue Ridge Parkway was America's first rural parkway. When ultimately completed it was also the nation's longest - 469 miles of uninterrupted mountain roads linking Shenandoah National Park in the north to the Great Smoky Mountains National Park in the south. The Blue Ridge Parkway is far and away the most popular destination in the National Park System - more than 19 million recreation visits per year. One of the explanations for its enduring popularity could be that the Blue Ridge is also one of America's most dog-friendly destinations. The nominees for the best hike with your dog along the Parkway are...

Black Balsam Knob (North Carolina)

"Balds" - where trees fail to grow - are found primarily in the Southern Appalachians, where the climate is too warm to support an alpine zone. Why some summits are bald and some are not is a mystery to scientists. There are two types of balds - heath balds with blankets of evergreen shrubs and grassy balds covered with dense swards of native grasses. Black Balsam Knob, at 6,214 feet, is the highest grassy bald in the Blue Ridge Mountains. The *Art Loeb Trail* trips across Black Balsam Knob and neighboring Tennant Mountain with two miles of unobstructed views.

Craggy Gardens (North Carolina)

There are many, many incredible views along the Blue Ridge Parkway but it will hard to convince your dog that the 360-degree panorama at Craggy Pinnacle is not the best. And the views aren't even the main reason Craggy Gardens is one of the must-stop pull-offs on America's favorite scenic roadway. There are no tall trees on top of this 5,892-foot mountain. Instead, the slopes are blanketed with blueberry, mountain laurel, and gnarly Catawba rhododendron bushes. The sweet birch trees that try and grow here are often twisted into grotesque shapes that make great photo-ops with your dog.

Linville Falls (North Carolina)

Linville Falls are so spectacular that trails go to five overlooks to get as many viewing angles as possible. These are the best and easiest water displays on the Blue Ridge Parkway. But don't expect to jump out of your vehicle, spy the falls, and get right back on the road as these sporty hikes will test your trail dog. *Erwin's View Trail* twists through a forest of virgin hemlock to views above the hydrospectaculars; the *Plunge Basin Trail* picks its way through thickets of rhododendron and mountain laurel to the base of the Linville River gorge.

Moses Cone Park (North Carolina)

Your best trail companion is used to barreling through narrow ribbons of thick woods and scampering over rocks - and no doubt loves it. But sometimes your dog wants to just kick back and feel like top dog of the manor while out trotting on a hike. That's what awaits at the ancestral summer home of Moses and Bertha Cone, built with Southern textile mill money in the 19th century. Twenty-five miles of finely crushed gravel carriage roads that make this Parkway stop doggie heaven for canine hikers.

Peaks of Otter (Virginia)

Thomas Jefferson once wrote, "The mountains of the Blue Ridge, and of these the Peaks of Otter, are thought to be of a greater height, measured from their base, than any others in our country." The country was young then and it was hard to know everything it contained; the man on the nickel still hadn't even purchased Louisiana yet. But as your dog picks their way up the *Sharp Top Trail*, gaining over 1,500 feet in just one-and-a-half miles he could very well concur with Mr. Jefferson. The first inn opened in the Peaks of Otter in 1834 and so many folks have beaten a path to the top of 3,875-foot Sharp Top that they don't even bother to blaze the trail. The other Peaks of Otter? That would be Harkening Hill (3,364 feet) and Flat Top (4,004 feet). Both have hikes to their summits as well, longer and not as popular.

"A bone to the dog is not charity. Charity is the bone shared with the the dog, when you are just as hungry as the dog."
-Jack London

And the Waggie for Best Canine Hike on the Blue Ridge Parkway goes to...

...Black Balsam Knob!

The views across Black Balsam Knob and Tennant Mountain would merit a Waggie even if they were bought with an arduous half-day hike with your dog but those miles-long 360-degree mountain-top views are purchased with only a short and scenic fifteen-minute climb to the ridgeline. As you roll along only a few hundred feet below the highest point east of the Mississippi River the Parkway poster child Looking Glass Rock is in near-constant view from the trail. Dogs can do the *Art Loeb Tail* at Black Balsam Knob as a linear out-and back for double the time on the ridgeline or drop off to close a hiking loop on the level *Investor Gap Trail*, an old logging road with springs pouring across it for refreshment. Matching canine hiking on Black Balsam Knob stride for stride in "wow" moments is the moderate climb to the Sam Knob summit, a heath bald found on the opposite side of the trailhead.

Best Canine Hike Under Big Trees

Hikes under giant sequoias and coastal redwoods - the largest trees on earth - are truly mystical. For dog owners these opportunities are extremely limited as the arboreal giants are clustered in our national and state parks. Nonetheless, some canine hikers will not be denied the majesty of these hikes and there are places where your dog can get closer to these magnificent trees than a car window...

Arcata Community Forest (California)
Arcata Ridge Trail

This second growth redwood forest in the City of Arcata is California's first municipally owned forest. Second growth means making do with "only" 250-foot high trees instead of 350 feet. Numerous short spurs off the *Arcata Ridge Trail* spine offer countless loop opportunities on a combination of wide, roomy roads and pick-your-way footpaths. The elevation in the well-lubricated redwood forest ranges from 250 feet to over 1,000 feet and will definitely get your dog's tongue to panting in stretches.

Olympic National Forest (Washington)
Quinault Rain Forest Trail

Two loops penetrate deep into an old-growth forest where firs and spruce can tickle 300 feet in height. Clubmoss draping branches and thick canopies suffocate the light on the forest floor of this four-mile canine hike. At one magical turn in the *Quinault Rain Forest Trail* you stand with your dog beneath all four titans of the Pacific rain forest - Western red cedar, Sitka spruce, Douglas fir and Western hemlock - growing in a row. Giant trees can often be seen growing in orderly rows. This is the result of their propagating on the mossy safety of large ancestors fallen on the forest floor. When the nurse logs decay completely their thriving wards are left with a distinctive hollow root pattern. The loop serves up a rushing waterfall and spends time at Quinault Lake as well.

Sequoia National Forest (California)
Boole Tree Trail

Converse Basin Grove is a giant sequoia graveyard. This area was once quite possibly the finest sequoia grove that ever was. Massive trees over 300 feet high were enthusiastically felled by loggers - often for little more than shingles. So many trees were taken that the area is known today as Stump Meadow. The 2.5-mile loop leads to a depression containing a rare survivor, the Boole Tree. Once thought to be the largest giant sequoia in the world more exacting measurements have since placed it eighth. But the 113-foot girth of this leviathan is the greatest of all giant sequoias. Unlike its cousins in the more manicured national parks the Boole Tree lives in such unruly surroundings you may not immediately identify it until your dog is dwarfed by its presence.

Sierra National Forest (California)
Shadow of the Giants Trail

Naturalist John Muir discovered this redwood grove in 1875 and as he investigated he happened upon a retired miner named John Nelder who was homesteading there. The area was heavily logged thereafter, mostly sugar pines, firs and cedar but the largest sequoias still stand. The self-guiding *Shadow of the Giants Trail* meanders for about a mile through the Nelder Grove. Unlike sequoias in national parks, the 100 giants here remain in dense forest and you can walk right up to the largest trees. Those would be Old Granddad and the Kids, a grouping of giant sequoias on a ridgeline and Bull Buck, one of the world's five largest arboreal monarchs at nearly 250 feet tall, 99 feet around at the base and probably 2700 years old.

Siskiyou National Forest (Oregon)
Oregon Redwoods Trail

The California-Oregon border wasn't drawn to give the Golden State all the redwood groves - it only seems that way. A sometimes harrowing four-mile dirt road leads to a considerably better maintained walking trail along and down Peavine Ridge on the *Oregon Redwoods Trail*. The grove of old-growth redwoods is interspersed with other upland forest species that permit enough light for huckleberry and rhododendron to flourish in patches. The largest redwoods are found after the 1.6-mile forest path switchbacks to the bottom of the ridge.

And the Waggie for Best Canine Hike Under Big Trees goes to...

...Arcata Community Forest!

The combination of easy access and spirited hiking AND dog-friendly is tough to beat. Don't let the active management of this redwood forest put you off, you won't even notice that it qualifies as one of only 20 in America to be designated a "Model Forest" for excellent forestry practices. Though you are not far from downtown Arcata or U.S. Highway 101 nearly 150 bird species have been found in these trees. A number of rare plants can be identified as well.

As for hiking, your dogs can spread out on the road-like main trail that sweeps under the towering redwoods and be challenged by the 800-foot elevation gains depending on the side trails you choose.

Although your eyes will be tilted upwards most of the hike don't neglect to soak in the verdant fern-encrusted understory, especially in springtime when the California lady slippers are in bloom.

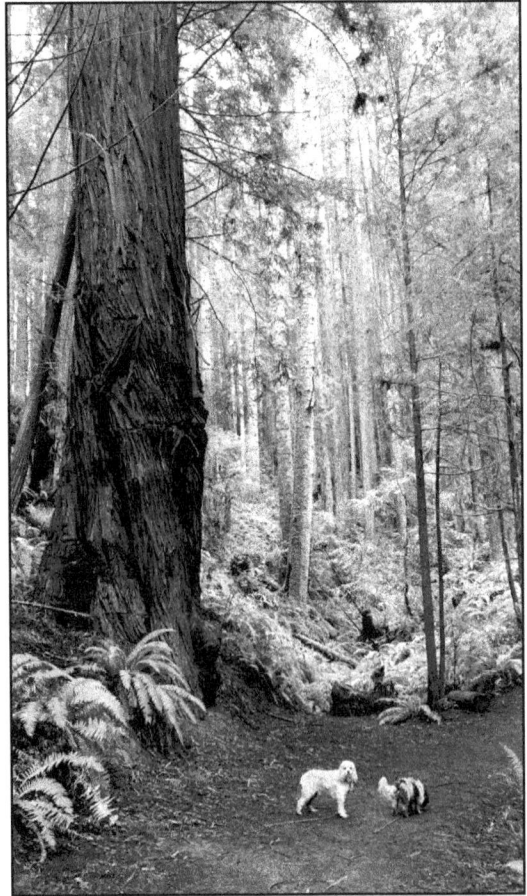

Best Canine Hike
in the Big City

You can't keep a trail dog down once they've seen the big city, especially in one of these Waggie-nominated parks...

Central Park (New York)

Chances are your dog will enjoy America's most famous park in midtown Manhattan as much as you will. Dogs are not allowed everywhere (Elm Islands at the Mall, Sheep Meadow, East Green, or Strawberry Fields are among the main prohibited areas) but can go off-leash before 9:00 a.m. where allowed. Keep an eye out for horses and city streets that cross the park. Architects Frederick Law Olmsted and Calvert Vaux designed the park to remain in a naturalistic setting so even in New York City you can lose yourself with your dog on woodland paths. And there's more elevation change than you might expect.

City Park (New Orleans)

Fifty percent larger than Central Park and many times wilder, City Park encloses an old bayou. It is also three years older than its New York cousin. The wide walking paths and trails meander under the world's

largest grove of mature live oaks, some of which were full-grown along the Bayou Metairie when the first French settlers arrived. There is off-leash time available in NOLA City Bark.

Fairmount Park (Philadelphia)

The largest contiguous landscaped municipal park in the world with nearly 9,000 acres began with just 5 acres in 1812. It is the bucolic home to an estimated 2,500,000 trees. The backbone of the park is the *Forbidden Drive*, so named when it was closed to automobiles in the 1920s. The 7-mile paved trail travels along the Wissahickon Creek to the Schuylkill River; canine hikes can be shortened by several bridges across the Wissahickon. In addition, there are many blazed single-track trails climbing steeply out of the Wissahickon Gorge.

Griffith Park (Los Angeles)

The seeds of one of the world's great city parks were sown with the arrival of Colonel Griffith Jenkins Griffith from Wales in 1865 to make his fortune in California gold mines. In 1882 Griffith came to Los Angeles and purchased 4,071 acres of an original Spanish land grant, Rancho Los Felix. In 1896 he gave more than 3,000 acres of California oaks, wild sage and manzanita to the city as a Christmas present - "a place of relaxation and rest for the masses." Today Griffith Park is the largest urban wilderness area in America, including 53 miles of trails, fire roads and bridle paths. Many of the trails feature views of the famous Hollywood sign - the *Mt. Hollywood Trail* climbs to the top.

Rock Creek Park (Washington DC)

Although technically a national park, Rock Creek Park is more like a city park administered by the National Park Service. How many other national parks boast of ballfields and 30 picnic sites? Two main parallel hiking trails, run the length of the park from north to south on either side of Rock Creek. The wiser choice for canine hikers is the *Valley Trail* (blue blazes) on the east side. In contrast with its twin, the *Western Ridge Trail* (green blazes), there are fewer picnic areas and less competition for the path. Each is a rooty and rocky frolic up and down the slopes above Rock Creek, a superb canine swimming hole. Numerous spur trails and bridle paths connect the two major arteries that connect at the north and south to create a loop about ten miles long.

And the Waggie for Best Canine Hike in the Big City goes to...

...Griffith Park!

The obvious recipient of the Waggie. If there was one essential canine hike of Americana it would have to be the hike to the Hollywood sign, wouldn't it? What was erected in 1923 as a billboard for selling houses and intended to stand for only 18 months is now the most recognizable icon of American culture to the rest of the world. The favored route to the Hollywood sign atop Mt. Lee is the *Canyon Drive Trail* because at its beginning your dog can pay homage to another Hollywood legend - the campy 1960s *Batman* television series. A short hike from the trailhead in the opposite direction leads to Bronson Caves, best known to Adam West fans as the entrance to the Batcave.

The trip to the Hollywood sign will cover 3.25 miles and gain nearly 1,000 feet in elevation, most on a steady climb. It is illegal to hike to the sign, perched safely behind restrictive fences, with or without your dog. Instead, the final steps to the summit wind behind the 50-foot high letters to the famous DOOWYLLOH view - Hollywood spelled backwards. Even without the sign, the panorama of Los Angeles and the Pacific Ocean from 1,708-foot Mt. Lee is amazing. A true American classic of a canine hike.

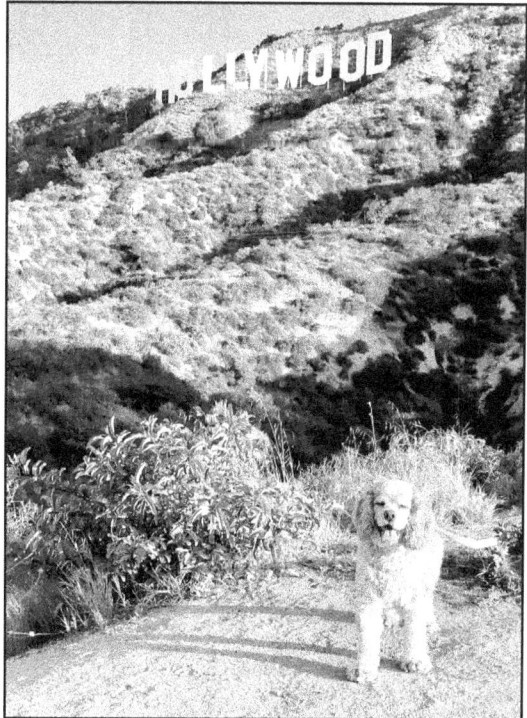

Best Canine Hike in
Sedona, Arizona

Sedona likes to call itself "the day hike capital of the country" and your dog will not bark in disagreement. More than 300 miles of non-motorized trails traverse the Red Rock Ranger District that surrounds the resort community. There are so many fantastic canine hikes in Sedona that any of five trails - Boynton Canyon, Cathedral Rock, Courthouse Butte Loop, Devil's Bridge or Fay Canyon - could win the Waggie. So many in fact that those five could be replaced by five others that could all win the Waggie. And let's do just that...

Airport Loop Trail

This loop circles Airport Mesa near the center of town for about 3.5 miles, picking up an elevation gain of over 200 feet in the journey. On view the entire way are Sedona's red rock landmarks in every direction - Elephant Rock, Bell Rock, Courthouse Butte, Cathedral Rock, the Sedona Pyramid, Chimney Rocks, Capitol Butte (the highest of Sedona's red rock peaks), Coffee Pot Rock, Steamboat Rock...well, you get the idea. They are all on display; about the only thing your dog won't see on the *Airport Loop Trail* is the airport.

Doe Mountain Trail

Doe Mountain, a flat top mesa in the western part of town, stakes its Waggie candidacy on views as well. The out-and-back affair gathers over 500 feet to the top and half of the 1.2 miles is easy going across the mesa. Keep going to the far end for 360-degree vistas of red rock country. You'll find fewer trail users making the ascent although the crowds are likely to increase later in the day to experience one of Sedona's best sunsets.

Little Horse Trail

The early going on *Little Horse Trail* rolls along an old jeep road in its early stretches through fragrant stands of juniper. A short detour leads to the photogenic Chapel of the Holy jutting out of the mountainside. The destination is Chicken Point at the base of the impressive "Madonna and the Nuns" spire rock formation after 1.5 miles. Stop and turn around along the way for iconic views of the Sedona landscape. Further exploring down the *Broken Arrow Trail* will lead to Submarine Rock - signature rocks are everywhere in Sedona. As a bonus, pools and small waterfalls enliven the Little Horse washes after a rain.

Soldier Pass-Jordan-Brins Mesa Loop

The *Soldier Pass-Jordan-Brins Mesa Loop* is one that starts right on the north edge of town, just up the road from the dog park. Despite the proximity to civilization this canine hike will quickly immerse trail tramps in the deep green juniper forest and brilliant red and orange rock formations for which Sedona is famous. The course pushes through the manzanita and velvet mesquite of the Red Rock Secret Mountain Wilderness before it bursts into the open. There are long, unobstructed views with your dog of noted landmarks - Coffee Pot Rock, Wilson Mountain, Steamboat Rock and others.

West Fork Trail

They say one million people a year come to hike the trails in Sedona - and this is the most popular trail in the Coconino National Forest. No doubt your dog will want to see what all the fuss is about. The *West Fork Trail* begins with a stroll through an historic apple orchard dating back to the 1880s. Then the level path visits the ruins of the Mayhew Lodge whose buildings were consumed in a fire in 1980. In its hey-day Hollywood stars like Clark Gable, Jimmy Stewart, and Maureen O'Hara all frequented the rustic cabins here. Shortly you reach the West Fork of the Oak Creek and canine hearts start to race. Oak Creek Canyon is a serpentine passageway under white limestone and red sandstone cliffs that soar over 1,000 feet high. Dogs will no doubt love the 13 crossings of one of the few year-round streams in the Sedona high desert. The canyon is 14 miles long but most people call it quits at three miles.

And the Waggie for Best Canine Hike in Sedona, Arizona goes to...

...Soldier Pass-Jordan-Brins Mesa Loop!

Right smack in the middle of town, this hike delivers a little bit of everything Sedona has to offer and a little bit extra in a four-mile trip. You get the red rocks, you get the juniper forests, you get the memory-searing views, and you get a dash of desert architecture in the town. After all there is no pretending you are in the middle of the wilderness in Sedona. You will have to chug to reach the top of the 5,099-foot grass-covered Brins Mesa - the Chamber of Commerce views have been aided by a devastating 2006 fire that burned away the trees from the flat-top promontory. This was a real soldier's pass in the days of the United States cavalry, attracted by a unique perennial water source that collects in the Devil's Kitchen, Sedona's largest sinkhole, and the Seven Sacred Pools that have been carved out of the ocher-colored sandstone.

Best Canine Hike
in Red Rocks

Nothing says the American West quite like red rocks. Trail dogs know they have had a grand time when they return to the trailhead with a fine dust of red powder caking their paws. There are certainly no losers among these canine hikes but one has to be declared a winner...

Garden of the Gods (Colorado)
Palmer/Siamese Twins/Scotsman Trails

The indigenous Ute Indians referred to this area of protruding, jagged red rocks as "the old red land." Jump off the asphalt - which most of the million or so annual visitors never leave - onto the natural surface *Scotsman Trail* and head south in relative isolation. Across the park road the *Siamese Twins Trail* leads to a unique formation with a window that looks directly at Pikes Peak. Away from the Central Garden the jagged sandstone peaks are highlighted by lush green pinyon-junipers and become even more photogenic. Most of this hike rolls easily through prairie grasslands and mountain shrub.

Dixie National Forest (Utah)
Red Canyon Trail System

Nestled between dog-unfriendly Zion and Bryce National Parks, the Red Canyon has been described as "the most photographed place in Utah." Get the camera ready and point your dog to the *Pink Ledges Trail* behind the Visitor Center. You will soon be up close with the brilliant red rock formations and the accenting dark green conifers. Launch a five-mile loop across the street that will bring trail dogs to the exposed perch of Buckhorn Point on the top of the red rock country world.

Palo Duro Canyon State Park (Texas)
Lighthouse Trail

The "Grand Canyon of Texas" is one of the largest in America, yawning for over 120 miles and reaching depths of 800 feet. Yet the classic Palo Duro canine hike has nothing to do with the canyon. Instead, point your dog towards the park's signature red rock formation, a multicolored 300-foot high pier of Trujillo sandstone known as the Lighthouse. The trail is a joy to trot on - smooth, hard-packed dirt and usually wide enough to handle a pack of trail dogs. The route follows dry washes and troughs between small hills as you gain an easy 900 feet in elevation over three miles.

Red Rock Canyon National Conservation Area (Nevada)
Calico Tanks Trail

The trail into the cracks of the Rainbow Mountain Wilderness begins conventionally before breaking down in a boulder-stuffed wash where your dog can bound up any favored route through the canyon. Near the end are tinajas, pockets of water in the bedrock that may contain seasonal water; not enough for dog-paddling perhaps but plenty welcome in the harsh Mojave Desert. The conclusion of the 1.25-mile ramble is a full view of the Las Vegas skyline in the distance. After a refreshing dip and a look at Sin City it is back to bouncing and scrambling 450 feet down the canyon.

Valley of Fire State Park (Nevada)
Fire Wave Trail

The red sandstone formations here look as if they actually melted and cooled in place. An American Automobile Club representative traveling on a primitive road through the area in the 1920s gave the valley its name. The go-to hike is the *Fire Wave Trail* that travels around a red rock wall and onto undulating rock hills of reds and yellows and pinks. As you cross this rock color palette there is a suggested trail marked by cairns but really the entire desert landscape is open and beckoning for exploration. The out-and-back adventure concludes after 1.2 miles at an ice cream shop of swirling scoop-like confections in the rocks.

And the Waggie for Best Canine Hike in Red Rocks goes to...

...Dixie National Forest!

When you claim to be "the most photographed place in Utah" you had better come with game and the *Red Canyon Trail System* brings enough to score a Waggie. These trails are why digital photography was invented - you couldn't carry enough rolls of film on this canine hike if you had to. The composite trail rambles through a wide valley, trading the bright red cliffs for golden colored rocks and crushed stone paths, with close up visits to fanciful hoodoos. As you climb out of the bowl and back into the red rocks the trail and landscape become otherworldly before finally reaching Buckhorn Point at 7800 feet. Views extend across the entire Sevier Valley. Finally heading back down, the stately Ponderosa pines serve up their own pleasures, growing against the bright red canyon walls. Pink-gold-white-red, all of Utah's Color Country gets billing on this hike with your dog.

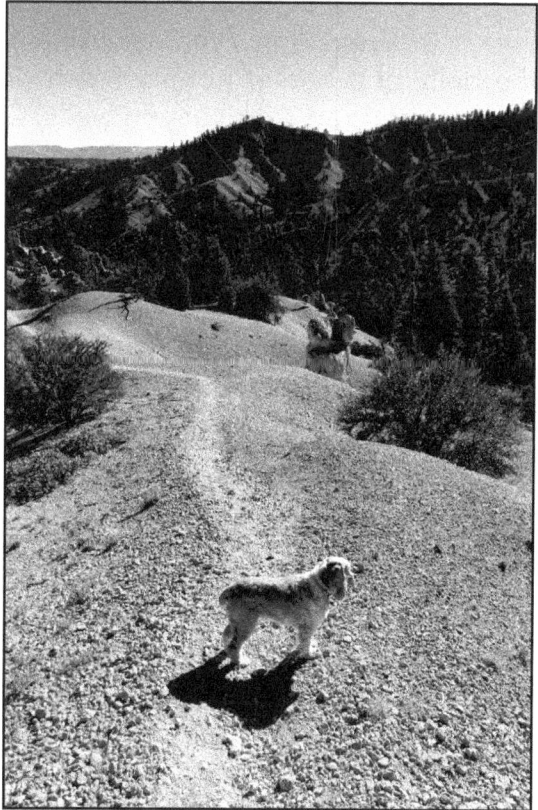

Best Canine Hike
through a Slot Canyon

A journey through a Southwest slot canyon - a fissure in the rock that begins as a tiny crack and grows larger through millenniums of occasional rushing water - are among the most memorable hikes your dog will ever take. Some slot canyons are roomy enough to handle a dog team, others constrict to passages narrower than a foot wide. Still more can be traversed only with ladders. The nominees for best Slot Canyon Canine Hike are all doable by any dog and owners with only average levels of claustrophobia...

Colorado Riverway Recreation Area (Utah)
Mary Jane Canyon

Professor Creek flows year-round, although seldom enough to reach the belly of a basset hound. Fresh green vegetation dances against the exposed red rock canyon walls. Canine hiking in Mary Jane Canyon (the professor's wife) begins almost from the parking lot and for the next four or so miles your dog will be splashing happily through the cooling desert stream waters. Eventually the winding canyon walls climb to over 100 feet and narrow to no more than 15 feet - if you haven't been hiking straight through the streambed the whole way you certainly will be here. The trail ends with a chokestone wedged into the canyon walls that produces an impressive 30-foot waterfall. The way out of Mary Jane Canyon is the same as the way in. There are numerous dry slot canyons on the sides to poke into along the way.

Crack Canyon Wilderness (Utah)
Little Wild Horse Canyon-Bell's Canyon

Little Wild Horse Canyon and neighboring Bell's Canyon can be combined to form a unique eight-mile loop that provides an ideal introduction to the Southwestern phenomenon of slot canyon hiking. Little Wild Horse Canyon is a classic slot canyon that narrows to single file passing in places with an obstacle or two to negotiate. Bell's Canyon is more airier but delivers gorgeous winding passages under high cliffs as well.

Grand Staircase-Escalante National Monument (Utah)
Willis Creek Canyon

At Willis Creek all that is required is to lock your vehicle and lead your dog into the slot canyon. There are no obstacles impeding your hike - save one, which can be bypassed - as the gorgeously sculpted walls close in down the creek. Those slickrock walls are streaked with desert varnish and will eventually grow to over 200 feet high deeper along. The wash-route trail is sand and cobblestones and mostly flat, gaining a nearly imperceptible 300 feet. When Willis Creek can't be avoided the water level is rarely deeper than splashing through a puddle. The narrow walls provide shade on even the hottest summer days. The dramatic twists and turns in Willis Creek slot canyon end after a little more than one mile as the wash yawns wider and canine hiking becomes more routine.

Paria Canyon-Vermilion Cliffs Wilderness Area (Utah)
Buckskin Gulch

Buckskin Gulch is the longest and deepest slot canyon in the Southwest. What it lacks in pretty walls and narrow passageways is made up in varying terrain. The canyon floor moves from soft sand to stone-speckled to rock-covered. Muddy pools, if present, will be your most challenging obstacle between these Navajo sandstone walls. Three trailheads modulate the length of time you will spend in the gulch with your dog, which can be considerable given the 12 miles of narrow walls.

Valley of Fire State Park (Nevada)
White Domes Canyon

At a little over one mile the White Domes packs plenty of excitement, especially if your dog is a Burt Lancaster or Lee Marvin fan since part of the Mexican hacienda set from the 1966 western *The Professionals* that was filmed here still remains along the trail. The sandstone walls narrow close enough to be touched by both hands for about 200 feet, traversed easily on a flat, gravelly wash. Nearby, at Wash No. 5, but unmarked on the map, the slot experience continues in Pastel Canyon with its maze of pinkish rocks and sand.

And the Waggie for Best Canine Hike through a Slot Canyon goes to...

...Crack Canyon Wilderness!

It's never easy to beat a two-fer deal, especially when the two slot canyons form a hiking loop. That loop can be tackled in either direction but clockwise (up Bell's Canyon to the the left first) seems to be the route of choice. A 1.5-mile jaunt along a wide jeep road links the two canyons through open desertlands and provides a refreshing break from the slots.

Saving Little Wild Horse Canyon for last negates a couple of the tougher rock scrambles and keeps the most exciting wiggles through the curvy passageways for last. The walls loom 300 feet high at this point. The canyon floor is flat and mostly dry but count on cold, brown water pooled dog-belly deep in spots as well. By the time your dog encounters the occasional chokestone in the slot they will realize this is a hike like no other, one that will surely be barked about in the dog park back home for a long time to come.

Best Canine Hike
to a Natural Arch or Bridge

All dogs know that flowing water is required to carve a hole through a rock wall to form a natural bridge, while an arch is freestanding and does not span a water course but for the purposes of awarding the Waggie we are not making a distinction. What matters is finding the best hike to one of these eye-catching natural wonders...

Alabama Hills Recreation and Scenic Area (California)
Arch Loop

"A fiery horse with the speed of light, a cloud of dust and a hearty Hi-Yo Silver! The Lone Ranger rides again!" Sorry, this is where the resourceful masked rider of the plains led the fight for law and order in the early western United States, as did more than 400 other Hollywood movies since the 1920s. In addition to being a movie set, the Alabama Hills, a jumble of rounded, weathered granite boulders piled across a desert flatlands that form a vibrant contrast with the sharply sculptured ridges of the nearby Sierra Nevada mountains, also is a swell place to hike with your dog. The stone-lined *Arch Loop* is the only formal hiking trail in the 30,000-acre Alabama Hills, leading to the twisted, personal-size Mobius Arch that provides a literal window directly to Mount Whitney, the tallest peak in the Lower 48. Stone steps tame the small arroyos along the way.

Big South Fork National River & Recreation Area (Tennessee)
Twin Arches Loop Trail

The Twin Arches form the largest sandstone arch complex in the East. The hollows are so thick with second-growth timber at Big South Fork that your dog will not even notice when the trail crosses the top of one of the massive natural bridges. Don't fret; there will be plenty of chance to appreciate these impressive arches from down below. Wooden steps help tame the steep descent into the rock houses. There are two loops to explore here; a 1.2-mile expedition to the arches and a full six-mile reconnaissance of the dark hollow. No doubt your dog will raise a paw to go for the whole tour.

Colorado Riverway Recreation Area (Utah)
Grandstaff Canyon Trail

There are more natural stone arches - over 2,000 - in Arches National Park than anywhere on earth. Your dog won't see any from beyond the parking lots, however. Luckily, just six miles from the park is a tail-friendly hike to the world's sixth longest natural arch and America's third longest. This canine hike pushes into Grandstaff Canyon, cut into Navajo Rock by an ancient stream emptying into the Colorado River. The packed-sand trail crosses the shallow-flowing stream many times as it works moderately uphill through the open canyon, especially in the last half-mile. A little more than two miles up into the canyon, pressed back against a rock wall, is multi-hued Morning Glory Natural Bridge that stretches 243 feet across a pool of water.

Coconino National Forest (Arizona)
Devil's Bridge Trail

Despite parking challenges (it gets crowded) and some steep climbs, the 4.2-mile out-and-back journey to see the Devil's Bridge is the most popular trail in Sedona. The early pawfalls are on a roomy trail but the going narrows as rock steps make the final ascent to the natural bridge. The hike ends above Devil's Bridge with an opportunity for dramatic photo-ops on top of the bridge itself. For a better canine hiking day skip the jeep road approach, at least on the return, and use the *Chuckwagon Trail* that features 360-degree views from rises in the red rock country.

Daniel Boone National Forest (Kentucky)
Auxier Ridge Trail/Double Arch Trail

Unlike most arches in the American West, the natural bridges in the Red River Gorge are tucked among a vibrant deciduous forest and are best viewed up close, often via a short trail from the scenic driving road. The more than 100 natural stone arches in the gorge represent the greatest collection east of the Mississippi River. Double Arch, with one opening on top of another, takes longer to reach than most, maximizing your dog's adventure in the rock formations.

And the Waggie for Best Canine Hike to a Natural Arch or Bridge goes to...

...Colorado Riverway Recreation Area!

This Waggie winner's name origins are almost as colorful as its hike. Back in the 1870s William Granstaff ran cattle in the canyon while he split up possession of the Spanish Valley with his erstwhile partner, a French-Canadian trapper known only as "Frenchie." Granstaff high-tailed out of the territory in 1881 when the law accused him of illegally selling liquor to local Indians. All he left behind was his name. The canyon was originally called Nigger Bill until the 1960s when it was rechristened "Negro Bill." Now, just last names suffice.

The sandy route picks its way through the abundant cottonwoods and willows thriving here until the canyon swings left and heads uphill across open slickrock. The canyon walls and the year-round stream make this a do-able canine hike even on a desert summer day. After two miles the multi-hued Morning Glory Natural Bridge appears, pressed back against a rock wall. Recent rains can transform the water hole under the arch into an ideal doggie swimming pool - watch for poison ivy, your dog won't be affected but will pass it on to you - before retracing your steps back to the parking area at the Colorado River.

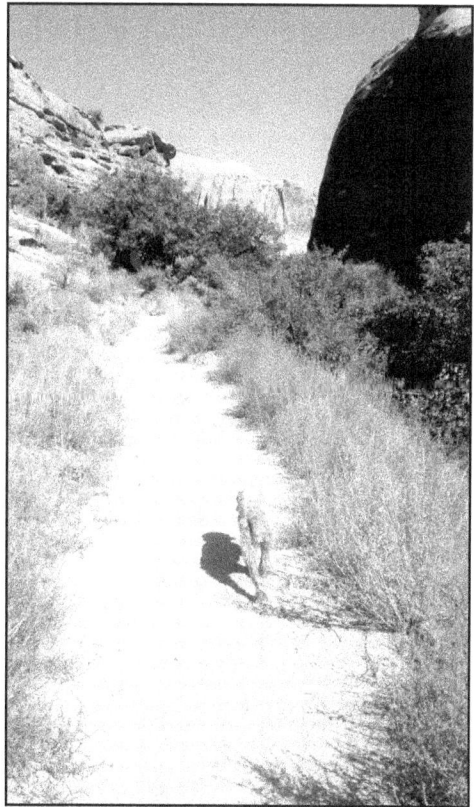

Best Doggie Playground in the American Southwest

The rock formations in the American Southwest are such an embarrassment of riches that rock gardens that would be a state park anywhere else don't even warrant a turnout in the highway. Some are more special than others, however, and the nominees for best place to open the car door and let your dog out to play are...

Bisti Wilderness Area (New Mexico)

The Bureau of Land Management busies itself more with mining claims and grazing rights than tourism promotion so the Bisti Badlands in the high desert of northwestern New Mexico are barely a blip on the canine hiker's radar. Thin layers of coal, silt, shale and mudstone in reds, blacks, browns, and tans conspire with more resistant sandstone to create hoodoos, clay hills, balanced rocks and small slot canyons. Petrified wood - sometimes complete stumps - and fossils abound. The alien world unfolds in a wide wash that runs for miles from the parking area.

Fantasy Canyon (Utah)

When you call yourself Fantasy Canyon you had better deliver the goods. This patch of photogenic eroded rocks does just that, with the added bonus that no axle-breaking drive is required to reach this remote slice of Northeast Utah. The canyon is tucked on the north side of a low mesa in the otherwise featureless expanse of the Uinta Basin. The gray-brown sandstone has eroded vertically and horizontally to fill a narrow ravine with fanciful delicate outcroppings. Fantasy Canyon earns its reputation as "nature's china shop" honestly. Someone has provided a name for 40 of nature's most intricate clay creations but you are likely to better enjoy seeing your own creatures in the formations..

Goblin Valley State Park (Utah)

The world didn't learn about this other-worldly place until the early 20th century when cowboys searching for cattle stumbled into the valley of weathered sandstone hoodoos and spires. The bizarre gnome-like rock formations spread out across a barren valley beneath the parking lot. Just point your dog down into Goblin Valley and head in any direction to start exploring this desert playground. Curious dogs will exalt in bounding up and around the orbital stones populating the valley floor. There are probably thousands of "goblins" living here. The edges of the valley feature intricately eroded cliffs and walls. Pushing beyond the main showcase, across intervening ridges, are more collections of hoodoos where the goblins are taller and more complex; you will still be encountering goblins two miles from the parking lot.

Grand Staircase-Escalante National Monument (Utah)
Devil's Garden

The Devil's Garden is off the beaten path, but not *too* far (12.3 miles from UT 12). It requires a trip down the notorious Hole-in-the-Rock Road but is passable by two-wheel vehicles to this point. And it delivers the multi-chromatic hoodoos, rock domes, and natural bridges all found in Utah's famous national parks, only in miniature. Devil's Garden has received a federal designation as an American Outstanding Natural Area. Explore the Navajo sandstone slickrock "garden" while keeping on the lookout for two signature arches, the delicate Metate Arch and the slab-like Mano Arch. Continue poking around until there are no more smoothed sandstone figurines and the garden tour is complete.

Grand Staircase-Escalante National Monument (Utah)
Toadstool Trail

Natural wonder and easy access are catnip for the traveling canine hiker. The *Toadstool Trail* checks both boxes big time. The canine hike starts from a parking lot directly on US 89 - the main road between Kanab, UT and Page, AZ - and leads into some of the most bizarre rock formations your dog will see in the American Southwest. The easy-going trail traces a sandy wash inside a broad canyon of white cliffs highlighted by chocolate brown rocks. In just under one mile you will spot your first "toadstool" - spire-like formations with a boulder perched on top of a pedestal rock. This introductory giant guardian is a poster child for many area travel brochures.

And the Waggie for Best Doggie Playground in the American Southwest goes to...

...Bisti Wilderness Area!

Apparently the four Utah playgrounds cannibalized each other's votes and the New Mexico wonderland takes the Waggie. But this is no compromise winner as hours of fun await dogs in the Bisti badlands. Canine hiking is always easy across a wide wash creased by tiny arroyos caused by rainwater. For spice, bound up and over the small clay hills that border the wash - and discover more topographical wonders beyond. Keep note of your position as Bisti lures canine explorers ever deeper into its nooks and rock gardens. There is always the feeling that your dog may be the first to sniff hidden discoveries.

Roam as you wish - there are no trails. The most common destination is to the southeast where a nursery of rocks that could double as alien space eggs reside about two miles out. Beyond that, logs and stumps of petrified wood begin in earnest. The main wash continues for miles with promises of a must-return visit.

Best Canine Hike through Antiquity

When Christopher Columbus "discovered" the Americas in 1492 there were already an estimated 75 million people living here, about the same population as in Europe. Today it is still possible to hike with your dog and see glimpses of these ancient civilizations...

Cahokia Mounds Historic Site (Illinois)
6.2 Mile Nature/Culture Trail

Cahokia was America's first metropolis, a cultural center constructed by the Mississippian Indians between 600 AD and 1200 AD that housed what is believed to have been as many as 20,000 people. These ancient "Mound Builders" dragged an estimated 50 million cubic feet of alluvial soil in baskets to construct over 100 ceremonial and functional mounds. Almost half of that dirt was used in building Monks Mound, the largest prehistoric earthen construction in the Western hemisphere. The *6.2 Mile Nature/Culture Trail* delivers what it promises with woodlands, meadows, and ponds while also visiting all the most important man-made treasures at Cahokia.

Effigy Mounds National Monument (Iowa)
Fire Point Trail

Cultures that inhabited the Mississippi region 2,500 years ago constructed mounds for religious, ceremonial, burial, and elite residential purposes. More than 200 mounds on these bluffs above the Mississippi River have have been documented in the monument, including 31 in the shape of spirit animals, or effigies. Nowhere have more been found. The *Fire Point Trail* is a two-mile canine hike that passes all four types of mounds: conical, linear, compound, and an effigy (Little Great Bear). Your dog will find a serious trail here as the dirt path switches to the top the bluffs. Panting tongues will recede after that.

El Morro National Monument (New Mexico)
Headland Trail

El Morro ("the Snout') is a prominent sandstone bluff that has been used as a wayfinding marker and campsite for 2,000 years. Ancestral Puebloans, Spanish, and American travelers have all etched signatures, dates, messages, and petroglyphs into the sides of El Morro. A pool of dependable water at the base of the cuesta offered a welcome oasis in the harsh landscape. The two-mile *Headland Trail* winds to the top of the bluff and takes your dog through the ruins of the pueblo of Atsinna, built around 1275 AD by the ancestors of the Zuni.

Ocmulgee Mounds National Historic Site (Georgia)
Bartram Trail/Opelofa Trail/Main Path

Ocmulgee Mounds hosted the largest archaeology dig in American history with over 800 men on site digging and discovering three million artifacts from over 17,000 years of habitation here. Eight miles of trails take in the Walnut Creek Wetlands, Civil War fortifications, and the Great Temple Mound, a 50-foot high structure utilized for religious ceremonies. Wooden stairs lead to the top and views of downtown Macon across the Ocmulgee River. Your dog can even walk into the Earth Lodge with its molded seats and 1000-year old floor.

Tonto National Monument (Arizona)
Lower Cliff Dwellings Trail

The cliff dwellings of the resourceful ancient inhabitants of the American deserts have long bred modern fascination, so much so that Mesa Verde in Colorado became the nation's seventh American national park and the first to "preserve the works of man" in 1906. The opportunities for your dog to explore cliff living are few but the *Lower Cliff Dwellings Trail* is one place to sneak a peek. Construction of the Upper and Lower Cliff Dwellings by the Salado culture began about 1300 CE and continued until the Tonto Basin was abandoned, between 1400-1450 CE. Some of the roofs of the cave architecture are original; signature saguaro cactus that dot the landscape were used as beams.

And the Waggie for Best Canine Hike through Antiquity goes to...

...Effigy Mounds National Monument!

These sacred grounds - no vehicles are permitted to mar the property - clinch the Waggie with 14 miles of self-guiding trails. Boasting some of the best scenic views of the Mississippi River anywhere, the monument also stakes a strong case for the best canine hiking in the state of Iowa. Certainly this is one of the few places in the Hawkeye State requiring switchbacks in the trail.

The Effigy Mounds resemble an English woodland park with a maintained grassy understory in the forest. The mounds are identified by higher grass. As the *Fire Point Trail* works its way to overlooks from hundreds of feet above the Great River there is no hurry to finish the loop. Atop the bluffs this agreeable canine hiking can continue to more scenic views and more effigies, including the Great Bear Mound Group, one of largest of its ilk.

"The greatest pleasure of a dog is that you may make a fool of yourself with him, and not only will he not scold you, but will make a fool of himself too."
- Samuel Butler

Best Canine Hike
on a Battlefield

America can be a strange place for dog owners. Places where you would not expect to be able to take your dog, like outdoor historic shrines, often welcome dogs on the grounds while places you would expect to be able to take dogs, like national parks, nearly all ban dogs. It almost feels like we have found a loophole in the system when we take our dogs to some of the most historic grounds in the country. The nominees for best canine hike across hallowed ground are...

Gettysburg National Military Park (Pennsylvania)

Gettysburg National Military Park, where Civil War Union forces halted a Confederate invasion commanded by Robert E. Lee, in south-central Pennsylvania, is America's most-visited battlefield. A good way for dog owners to digest the most analyzed three days in American history (July 1-3, 1863) - and escape the crowds - is to leave the auto tour and explore the grounds on foot. The battlefield swallows the town of Gettysburg although most of your walking will take place in quiet farmland and boulder-studded hillsides south of the village where the climactic fighting took place. A full day to hike with your dog can be crafted on the 9-mile *Billy Yank Trail* and the 3.5-mile *Johnny Reb Trail*.

Harpers Ferry National Historic Park (Maryland)

No place in America packs as much scenic wonder and historical importance into such a small area as Harpers Ferry National Historic Park where the Shenandoah and Potomac rivers join forces. George Washington surveyed here as a young man. Thomas Jefferson hailed the confluence as "one of the most stupendous scenes in Nature" and declared it worth a trip across the Atlantic Ocean just to see. U.S. Marine Colonel Robert E. Lee captured abolitionist John Brown here. Stonewall Jackson scored one of his greatest military victories here during the Civil War. Even Meriwether Lewis and his dog Seaman showed up in Harpers Ferry to get arms for the Corps of Discovery. The Maryland Heights is where you can see it all, rising ruggedly from the canal towpath to 1,448 feet above the rivers.

King's Mountain National Military Park (South Carolina)

Thomas Jefferson called it, "the turn of the tide of success." For the British, Sir Henry Clinton called the defeat at Kings Mountain, "the first link in a chain of evils that at last ended in the total loss of America." Revolutionary War buffs will certainly make the pilgrimage to Kings Mountain, site of some of the most vicious American vs. American fighting of the war on October 7, 1780. You can hike with your dog on an interpretive walking trail around Battlefield Ridge, through the thickly wooded mountainside that provides an excellent feel for what fighting must have been like on that critical day in the American Revolution.

Pea Ridge National Military Park (Arkansas)

Dogs are welcome throughout Pea Ridge, the first battlefield west of the Mississippi River to be declared a national military park. It is also the largest. The seven-mile hiking loop travels through fields and woodlands - a splendid natural romp for your dog with an overlay of pivotal American history. The trail visits skirmish sites of the March 1862 Union victory, rock outcroppings with small caves, building foundations and quiet stream beds, small sandstone canyons, zigzag split-rail fences, and flowering dogwoods. There is enough challenge to hiking the Pea Ridge battlefield to set your dog to panting and long stretches where they can bask with sunlight on the neck.

Saratoga National Historic Park - (New York)

Saratoga is one of the most famous and influential battlefields in world history. In two battles, three weeks apart in the fall of 1777, American general Horatio Gates pounded British commander John Burgoyne who was awaiting reinforcements that never arrived. The surrender of 6,000 British regulars guaranteed the Colonies would not be split along the Hudson River and went a long way towards gaining American independence. The National Park Service maintains this ground much as it looked more than 240 years ago. On the *Wilkinson National Recreation Trail* your dog with follow a 4.2-mile balloon loop that travels on roads used by the British during the two battles. Saratoga isn't just walking in the footsteps of Revolutionary War soldiers - it's a Waggie-nominated canine hike.

And the Waggie for Best Canine Hike on a Battlefield goes to...

...Harpers Ferry National Historic Park!

Wayside exhibits on the *Stone Fort Trail* give an appreciation of the effort involved in dragging guns, mortar, and cannon up the 1,448-foot mountainside to a commanding position overlooking the three states that converge at Harpers Ferry. Just one 9-inch Dahlgren gun capable of lobbing 100-pound shells weighed 9,700 pounds. The wooded trail leads to the remnants of the Stone Fort which straddles the crest of Maryland Heights at its highest elevation. Even without pulling heavy ordnance on the steep and rocky trail your dog will welcome the stops at scenic overlooks and understand how this hike wins a Waggie. Back on the towpath, a footbridge across the Potomac River leads to Lower Town in Harpers Ferry - accessible otherwise only by a dog-unfriendly shuttle bus.

Best Canine Hike
at an Old Fort

The first thing European settlers did when they arrived on our shores was build a fort. From these crude wilderness earthworks and log blockhouses to the massive masonry fortifications of the 19th century, forts played a key role in the American story. Many of the old forts remain wholly or partially intact, original or restored, and make unique destinations with your dog. The nominees for the best are...

Fort Bowie (Arizona)

Fort Bowie was the operations center for the U.S. Army's actions against the Chiricahua Apaches for more than two decades; it was located to protect the perennial waters of Apache Springs. The conflicts culminated in the surrender of medicine man and tribal leader Geronimo in 1886. The fort was abandoned in 1894. The wooden timbers were salvaged by local ranchers and miners and the lands sold off at public auction for a couple of dollars an acre. Modern life hasn't gotten very close to the Fort Bowie ruins in the past century and the only public way in is a 1.5-mile trail that mixes high desert landscapes with lush, riparian woodlands.

Fort Fisher (North Carolina)

The largest earthwork fort in the Confederacy was constructed here to keep Wilmington's port open to blockade runners during the Civil War. The Union did not feel confident enough to assault Fort Fisher until December 24, 1864. For two days the sand and earth fortifications absorbed gunboat shells until Northern forces withdrew. On January 12 a bombardment by land and sea finally produced a white flag after six hours of fierce fighting. It was considered the greatest land-sea battle of the Civil War and helped seal the ultimate fate of the Confederacy. Earthworks still remain at the historic site that is now a recreation area. The *Basin Trail* slips almost unnoticed from the south end of the fort into what appears to be a maritime forest. Your dog will twist through a maze of wax myrtles for only a few steps, however, before bursting into the open with nothing ahead but a stretch of seven miles of tail-friendly, dune-backed sand beaches.

Fort Abraham Lincoln (North Dakota)

When a collection of military posts at the confluence of the Missouri and Heart rivers were formalized into Fort Abraham Lincoln in 1872 Lieutenant George Armstrong Custer was named first post commander. Four years later when Custer headed west to the Little Bighorn in Great Sioux War, this is where he rode out from. In 1907 Fort Abraham Lincoln became North Dakota's first state park. Custer's house and several fort buildings are the pushing off point for seven miles of some of America's best prairie grass canine hiking in the hills above the Missouri River with views to the state capital in Bismarck.

Fort Robinson (Nebraska)

With more than 22,000 acres, Fort Robinson is one of Nebraska's largest recreation areas. There is also plenty of canine history for your dog to honor here. The military post was established in 1874 and evolved into the world's largest facility for training horses and mules for cavalry forces. During World War II the country's K-9 Corps training center was established at Fort Robinson. More than 14,000 dogs were prepped for military duty and civilian service here. Today's dogs can hike through a land of eroded buttes and bluffs that make ideal doggie resting spots to soak in the vast grasslands and history spreading beneath the *Smiley Canyon Loop Trail*.

Fort Snelling (Minnesota)

The Dakota Indians considered the spot at the confluence of the Minnesota and Mississippi rivers the center of the world; European visitors recognized its strategic importance for trade and defense. The standout hike among 18 miles of trails at Fort Snelling is the loop around Pike Island. This is easy trotting under the biggest trees in the Twin Cities area with plenty of opportunity for swim-loving canine enthusiasts to play in the water. The wide, crushed gravel paths cover a 3.2-mile circuit with cut-off options for shorter hikes and access to the interior. At the far point of the loop the Minnesota River flows memorably into the Mississippi River for its journey through America's heartland.

And the Waggie for Best Canine Hike at an Old Fort goes to...

...Fort Bowie!

Fort Bowie grabs the Waggie for best creating frontier 19th century American life in a fort - the only way in is by the 1.5-mile footpath through a pass in the Dos Cabezas Mountains to the north and the Chiricahua Mountains guarding the south. The route was scouted for a Transcontinental Railroad and rejected. The canine hike visits the ruins of the Butterfield Overland Mail Station, the Fort Bowie Cemetery, and the still reliable Apache Springs before reaching Fort Bowie and the adobe remnants of about 40 outpost buildings. After your dog pokes around the echoes of military history make sure to find the *Overlook Look Trail* (behind the remote visitor center) for the return trip. The rocky ledges serve up long mountain views among chaparral spiced with soaptree yucca, ocotillo, and a variety of cacti. The elevation gain of about 700 feet comes easily through the transitional life zone between the hot and dry Sonoran Desert and the milder Chihuahuan Desert.

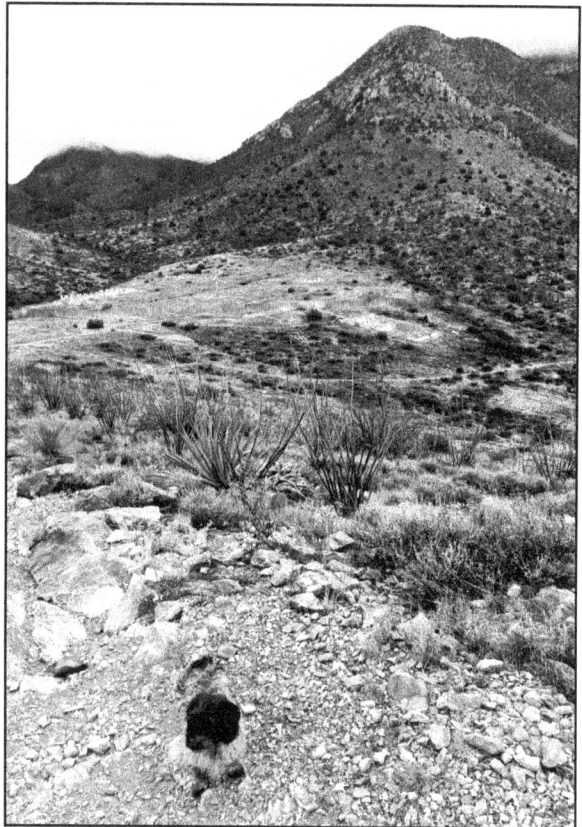

Best Canine Hike
through a Ghost Town

When you go hunting ghost towns with your dog you will find that "ghost" is a broad term. Some ghost towns still have a handful of people living in them; others are tourist attractions with actors and gift shops. These Waggie-nominated ghost towns are administered by state and federal governments as parks and look more or less the way they looked when the last resident left......

Bannack (Montana)

The town of Bannack once boasted 3,000 citizens and was the first territorial capital of Montana. Gold in Grasshopper Creek was its lifeblood and the riches did not play out completely until the 1950s. The population trickled steadily away during that time until the town was completely abandoned. Since then the state has maintained 60+ structures in the remote valley in a state of arrested decay. Your dog can walk through the ghost town streets and even into the empty buildings. Some, like the School House and stately Hotel Meade appear like they could be in operation tomorrow; others feature peeling asbestos floor tile and crumbling ceilings. Go inside any building that is not locked - just remember to close the door on your way out.

Bodie (California)

Bodie is the best preserved, most extensive ghost town where you can hike the streets with your dog. William Bodey dug gold out of these barren hills in 1859 but he died in a blizzard that winter and never saw the town his strike - one of the richest in California history - would spawn. By 1880 Bodie was bustling with 10,000 residents. This is no tourist trap - there are no re-creations in Bodie and no food and water for sale. The only business that intrudes on the ghost town aura is a small museum. You can walk your dog into the gravelly streets of the townsite with 170 documented buildings, peering into store windows with shelves still stocked and pool halls with balls still racked on dusty, ornate tables. Bodie sits at 8,375 feet so your dog will get a workout hiking into the hills on the outskirts of town to see the cemetery, the stamp mill, and other boomtown relics.

Elkhorn (Montana)

Elkhorn boomed behind the discovery of silver by Swiss-born Peter Wys in 1870. Over the years almost nine million ounces of silver were extracted from Elkhorn Mine. After the railroad arrived in 1887 it was estimated that more than $30,000 a day worth of silver was being shipped out of Elkhorn. When the silver market crashed in the 1890s most of the people living in the town and nearby gulches moved on to the next strike. A handful of people still live in Elkhorn and most of the buildings are privately owned but you are welcome to visit and follow the self-guided walking tour with your dog. Elkhorn Ghost Town State Park preserves two outstanding examples of frontier architecture side-by side: Fraternity Hall and Gillian Hall.

Rhyolite (Nevada)

When quartz - an indicator of gold - was found all over a hillside in 1904 there were soon 2,000 claims in a 30-mile radius of the town of Rhyolite. Soon the population approached 10,000; the railroad arrived and the town was electrified. There were hotels, a hospital, a school for 250 children, a stock exchange and even an opera. The financial Panic of 1907 decimated the town and by 1916 the lights and power were turned off forever in Rhyolite. The "Queen City" of Death Valley barely lasted a decade. The old mining town fulfills every image your dog has ever had of a ghost town in a stark, wind-whipped desert with the feeling that no dog has sniffed these streets in years. Aside from being remote Rhyolite is amazingly accessible - a paved road motors straight into town.

South Pass City (Wyoming)

South Pass brought emigrants along the Oregon Trail and gold dis-covered in the the surrounding Wind Mountains in 1867 spurred the development of this frontier mining town. After the ore played out the population steadily dwindled until by 1949 only buildings were left in the folds of the mountains. The state restored 30 of the original 250 buildings and South Pass City is one of the most authentic and com-plete historic sites in the country. Besides the wide dirt Main Street the grassy trails around town lead to gentle streams, a gold-crushing stamp mill, and a collection of residential cabins and rock houses.

And the Waggie for Best Canine Hike through a Ghost Town goes to...

...Bannack!

It is one thing to walk back in time with your dog down the street of a ghost town but opening a door and walking inside wins a Waggie. The sixty or so log and frame structures are remarkably well-preserved, many of them two stories and boasting the latest architecture of the day.

There is an opportunity for canine hiking beyond the town site. A trip up Hangman's Gulch leads your dog to the site of the gallows and the nearby cemetery where the first gold hunters were buried in 1862. Trotting down the road east of town winds through a broad canyon and to the site of the Hendricks Mill where Bannack gold - 99% pure compared to the typical 95% - was processed. The round-trip for this easy exploration is just short of three miles.

Another hiking loop south of the Bannack townsite follows an old stage road into the hills for views of wildflowers and the old mining community, one of America's best preserved ghost towns.

Best Canine Hike through a Tunnel

Trail dogs are naturally curious and nothing sets tails to wagging like the prospect of a big, dark tunnel ahead on the trail. With America's energetic Rails-to-Trails conversion movement many unique opportunities to hike with your dog through tunnels have sprouted in recent years. Let's take a look at the nominees for the best and remember to bring your flashlight...

Black Hills National Forest (South Dakota)
Flume Trail #50 - Loop A

The two square-timbered tunnels on this National Recreation Trail weren't constructed in the 1880s for trains but for water. The wooden flume carried water 20 miles from Spring Creek to placer mines that eventually washed $20 million in gold from the diggings. Eleven miles of the trail follow the original Rockerville Flume through prime Black Hills scenery, with long stretches of canine hiking in the actual bed. That includes the stout tunnels, dark and damp just like an adventurous dog wants.

Caprock Canyons State Park (Texas)
Trailway

Some 17.5 miles of abandoned Fort Worth and Denver Railroad tracks between Estelline and South Plains have been converted to recreational use. The highlight of canine hikes on this largely dirt trail is the Clarity Tunnel, 4.5 miles from the nearest trailhead at Monk's Crossing to the east. Built in 1922, this was the last active railroad tunnel in the Lone Star State. Today it is dark enough to house a summer colony of 500,000 Mexican free-tailed bats.

Chesapeake & Ohio Canal National Historic Park (Maryland)
Paw Paw Tunnel Trail

Rosy-eyed planners began work on this canal tunnel in 1836 with a goal of 7-8 feet gained a day. Instead, the pace was more like 12 feet a week. Fourteen years and six million bricks later the 26-foot high tunnel was opened. One of the most unique hikes you can take with your dog starts in a national park service campground and travels a short distance on the well-maintained towpath of the canal until you reach the 3,118 Paw Paw Tunnel where your dog will be plunged into complete darkness.

Florida Caverns State Park (Florida)
Visitor Center Trail

What, you say, a tunnel in Florida where the average elevation is 12 feet above sea level? Not a man-made one but the *Visitor Center Trail* that winds through a fairy garden of whimsical limestone formations includes a stretch where your dog embarks on a unique underground adventure through Tunnel Cave.

Lake Mead National Recreation Area (Nevada)
Historic Railroad Trail

The old railroad bed goes through not one, not two, but five tunnels in the course of a little over two miles. The tunnels were blasted in 1931 to bring supplies to the building site of Hoover Dam. To accommodate the bulky equipment and large penstocks being hauled the tunnels are each 25 feet in diameter and left unfinished, save for some wooden vertical supports at the entrances. The longest are the length of a football field - enough to enter near darkness. The railroad shut down in 1961.

And the Waggie for Best Canine Hike through a Tunnel goes to...

...Lake Mead National Recreation Area!

The only thing as impressive as these massive railroad tunnels are some of the area's best views of Lake Mead, the largest reservoir ever completed in the United States. Those views come with almost no purchase as the elevation gain on this two-mile trail is only 11 feet. To make this ramble through five tunnels with your dog even more pleasurable the entire road grade was refinished with paw-friendly decomposed granite in 2017. The tunnels, spaced at intervals, provide a cool respite from a hot desert day. And expect this to be a very social doggie hike most times of the year. As an added bonus, for budget-minded canine hikers the *Historic Railroad Trail* is outside the Lake Mead NRA entrance gate. The only doggie downer is that the trail continues after the fifth tunnel to views of the monumental Hoover Dam but dogs are not permitted.

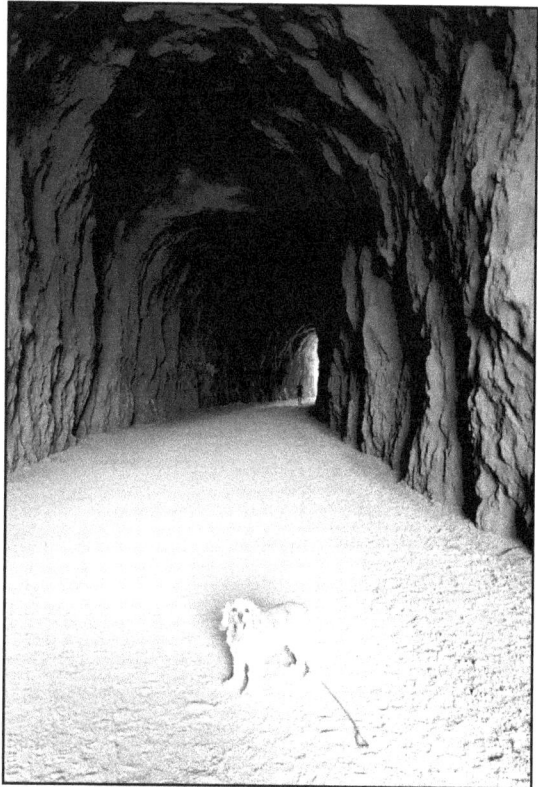

Best Canine Hike
at School

There are more good times for your dog than graduate level puppy classes at America's colleges and universities. Many a campus is dog-friendly and here are the nominees for the best hike with your dog at school...

Cornell University (New York)
Cornell Botanic Gardens

With grounds sprawling across more than 3,500 acres, the Cornell campus hosts one of the top five largest botanic gardens in North America, roomy enough to visit gorges and gardens, wetlands and woodlands. More than 50,000 plants live here. The F.R. Newman Arboretum is routinely recognized as one of the most beautiful curated tree museums in the United States. The trails are divided between cultivated collections and natural areas that double as outdoor classrooms and the heavy focus on academics is likely to rub off on your dog.

Harvard University (Massachusetts)
Arnold Arboretum

The Arboretum was founded in 1872 when the President and Fellows of Harvard College became trustees of a portion of the estate of James Arnold, a New Bedford whaler in the early 1800s. Today, Boston's tree museum spreads across 265 acres where more than 15,000 trees, shrubs and vines grow under the careful eye of the Arboretum's plant stewards. There is no prettier hike you can take with your dog in Massachusetts. Designer Frederick Law Olmsted's trademark paths curve gently across the property and before you know it your dog has reached the top of Peters Hill with one of the city's best vistas playing out before him among the gingkos and honey locust trees. Or peering through the lilac collection at the Boston city skyline on Bussey Hill.

"If your dog is fat, you aren't getting enough exercise."
- Anonymous

Mississippi State University (Mississippi)
Crosby Arboretum

The Lucius Olen "L.O." Crosby family, the largest timber industrialists in Mississippi, created the arboretum in the 1980s. Even though it is a mere sapling among its fellow plant conservators agewise Crosby Arboretum has piled up local and national awards. The collection is considered the South's premier native plant conservatory as it preserves and displays all three habitats found in the Southern ecosystem: woodland, savanna, and aquatic. Your dog is welcome to explore all 104 acres of longleaf pine forest, hillside bogs, bald cypress-tupelo swamps, and slash pine hardwoods.

Swarthmore College (Pennsylvania)
Scott Arboretum

The 300-acre Swarthmore campus is developed to be an arboretum, established in 1929 as a living memorial to Arthur Hoyt Scott, Class of 1895. Stop in the office to pick up a tour map to the Scott Arboretum collections that are integrated with the stone buildings of the college that date to 1864. A dog-friendly campus, you'll find dog water bowls at the drinking fountains as you travel among the 4,000 different kinds of plants. You can finish your tour in Crum Woods where your dog can go under voice control on the rolling dirt paths, swim in Crum Creek and even visit Swarthmore's version of Stonehenge.

University of Washington (Washington)
Washington Park Arboretum

Hugging the glacially carved Lake Washington, the Arboretum has built an international reputation for its collection of oaks, conifers, camellias, Japanese maples, and hollies. Designed by the Olmsted Brothers in 1934, these 230 acres are considered to be Seattle's first park. The Union Bay Natural Area and Yesler Swamp, comprising one of the largest remaining wetlands on the lake, feature tail-friendly walking trails with long views of the water.

"The best thing about a man is his dog."
-French Proverb

And the Waggie for Best Canine Hike at School goes to…

…Mississippi State University!

The Pinecote Pavilion, a symmetrical shed, resting on a base of earth-toned brick, surrounded by earth, water, and trees designed by Frank Lloyd Wright acolyte Fay Jones, is the perfect home for Crosby Arboretum's new Waggie. Jones also designed bridges and other elements in the tail-wagging trail system that welds a dozen short paths together in a series of stacked loops. The soft dirt and sand trails are a delight under paw as they visit ponds and savannas and nutrient-starved bogs where carnivorous pitcher plants thrive. Crosby supports over 300 different species, including several rarities. Your dog can cobble together over three miles of shady hiking here, even approved for hot Southern summer outings.

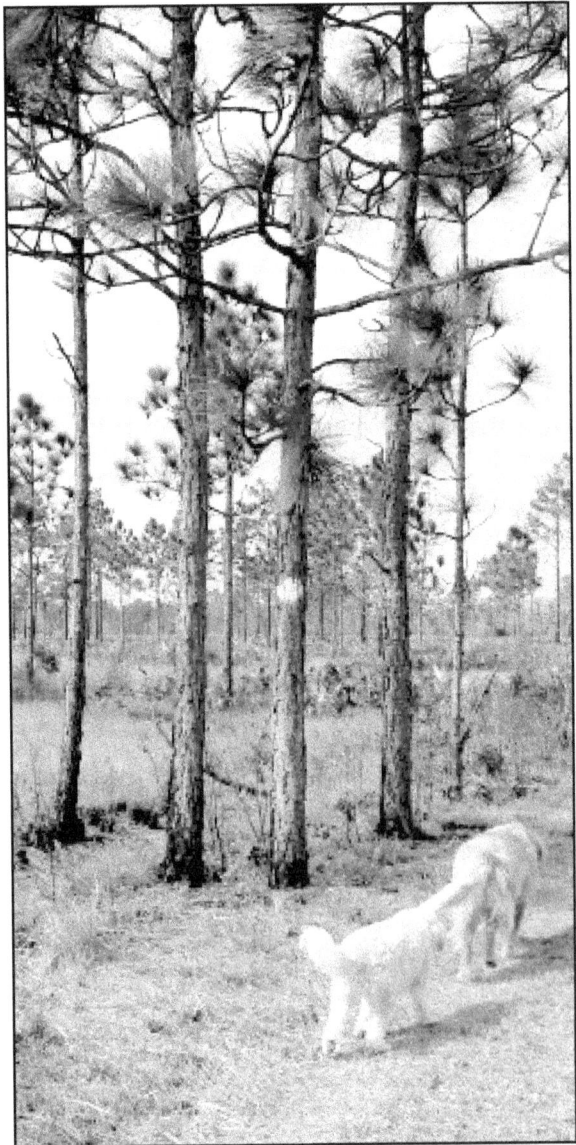

Prettiest Canine Day Hike

Experienced travelers know there are attractions you drive right by with your dog's nose pressed forlornly against the car window. Formal gardens are typically high on the list of places that do not allow dogs. But not so fast - there are nominees for best garden hike with your dog...

Boyce Thompson Arboretum (Arizona)

Boyce Thompson was born in Montana, educated in New England, and made his fortune trading mining stocks in New York City but it was the desert landscape of the American southwest that captured his heart. In the 1920s he established the arboretum to study the plants of desert countries and invited the public to share in the research. Today more than 3,200 desert plants are interspersed amidst two miles of winding, pebbly paths, which your dog is welcome to enjoy. Where water intrudes on the 320-acre garden in the form of a man-made lake or trickling stream the impact is startling. Shade-giving eucalyptus trees share space with majestic 200-year old saguaro cactus, Chinese pistachio trees are neighbors to spiky palo-verdes and Mediterranean olive trees compete for attention with spiny-branched ocotillo.

Callaway Resort & Gardens (Georgia)

Cason Callaway drove hard to make his family's cotton mill and retail business until a heart attack at the age of 54 forced him to slam on the brakes. He segued into the less stressful world of gardening but in Callaway fashion was soon planning and planting 2,500 Pine Mountain acres. The tail-friendly wooded trails wind gently across the property that is dominated by a string of lakes. The prize specimens are the 700 species of azalea that explode into bloom each spring.

Holden Arboretum (Ohio)

After graduating from Harvard with a degree in Mining Engineering in 1888, Albert Fairchild Holden joined his father in the silver fields of Utah. He later bought his father's mines and organized the United

States Mining Company to consolidate his expanding interests. Soon he was smelting more ore than anyone in the country and founded the Island Creek Coal Company in West Virginia to supply his furnaces. Albert Holden died of cancer in 1913 but endowed today's "tree museum" that has grown into one of the world's largest arboretums with more than 6,000 varieties of plants and trees spread over 3,446 acres.

Magnolia Plantation and Gardens (South Carolina)

How dog-friendly is Magnolia Plantation? Not only are dogs allowed to walk the grounds but they can ride the tour trams and even go in the plantation house (if you carry your dog). And it is quite a treat - you are not likely to have a canine hike like this anywhere else. The prescribed path through the maze of walking paths stops at two dozen points of interest, crosses graceful bridges, looks in on 250 varieties of azaleas, skips through quiet stands of towering bamboo and wanders by 900 types of camellias. More canine hiking is available through the 60-acre blackwater cypress and tupelo swamp. Plus there are nature trails on the property.

National Arboretum (Washington, D.C.)

The United States Department of Agriculture established the National Arboretum as a research and education facility and living museum in 1927. Dogs are permitted across the grounds, which include a mix of tree collections and formal gardens. The major trail system circles Mount Hamilton, at 240 feet one of the highest points in the nation's capital. A paved road/path winds to the top where you can peek through the trees to the west and see the U.S. Capitol and the Washington Monument. On the southern and eastern slopes are over 15,000 hardy azaleas that can still see blooms into November. Your dog can stroll through gardens devoted to perennials, to herbs and to energy-producing plants and across a meadow containing twenty-two carved sandstone Corinthian columns that once stood at the east portico of the U.S. Capitol.

And the Waggie for Prettiest Canine Day Hike goes to...

...Holden Arboretum!

Holden Arboretum takes the Waggie with more than a dozen paw-friendly trails, ranging from garden strolls to meadow romps to mature woodland hikes for your dog. The trails curve pleasingly among the plantings, often visiting the edges of ponds. Energetic dogs will want to push to the park's extremities on the sporty *Pierson Creek Loop* and *Bole Woods Trail* that explore a stunning beech-maple forest, designated a National Natural Landmark. In the southern region the Conifer collection is an evergreen wonderland any month of the year. You may be distracted by the beauty of the place and not notice as you hike but your dog can get quite a workout in Holden Arboretum, with several hundred feet of elevation changes. Woodcarver Dan Sammon used chainsaw and torch to create "The Guardians of the Garden" in the base of a toppled 275-year old red oak.

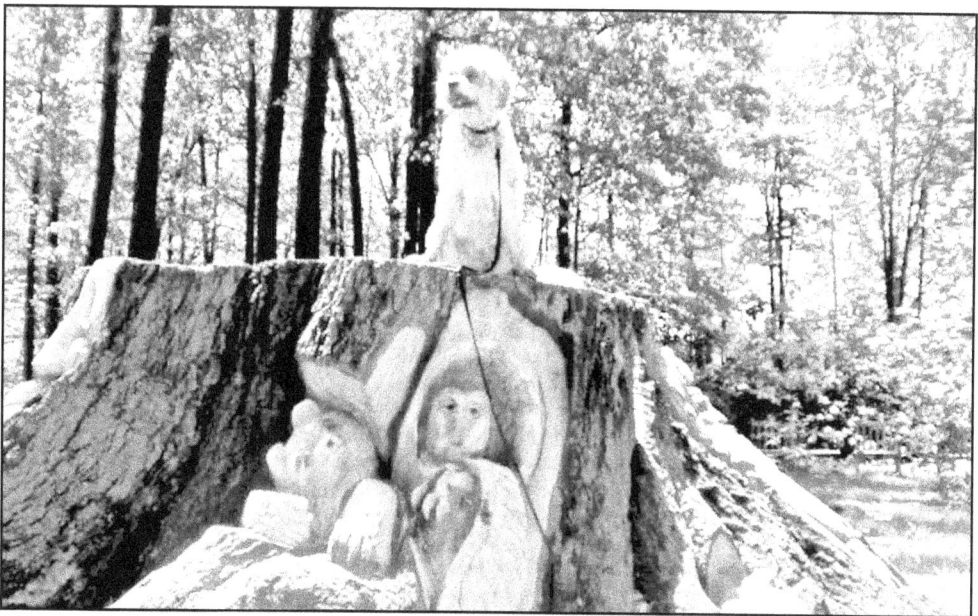

Best Canine Hike
In America

Forget the nominees. Dispense with the envelopes. The Waggie for Best Canine Hike in America goes to **Minnewaska State Preserve Park** on New York's Shawangunk Mountain Ridge. It was in this wild and rocky wilderness 2,000 feet above sea level that feuding brothers Alfred and Albert Smiley opened competing vacation houses in the 1800s. When they made nice again the Smileys built a network of 35 miles of carriage roads between the hotels. These wide, carefully graded roadbeds link a trio of dramatic sky lakes, plunging waterfalls, and lush woodlands. But it is the sheer cliffs and ledges that your dog will best remember here. If your best trail companion could talk you would hear about this hike for a looooong time.

Several long parallel carriageways between Lake Awosting and Lake Minnewaska can be combined for loop hikes of several hours duration. For spectacular views of the Hudson Valley use the *Castle Point Carriageway* to Castle Point, the highest summit in the park. Looks at the Catskill Mountains come quickly on the short, steep Sunset Path near the entrance parking lots. The narrow hiker-only paths are where the adventure begins for canine hikers at Minnewaska State Park Preserve. These trails are generally moving up and down, leading to treasures deep in the Shawangunks like Stony Kill Falls.

The early steps on the ramble to Gertrude's Nose in the Gunks lead to a swimming beach at cliff-fringed Lake Minnewaska. If this was as far as your dog went it would probably be a four-star hike. The *Millbrook Mountain Carriage Road* then moves through mixed forests onto the open cliffs and Patterson's Pellet, a glacial erratic

perched improbably on the edge of a cliff.

The carriage road joins *Gertrude's Nose Trail*, a beguiling footpath that will eventually spend much of its 2.7 miles poking along flat, open clifftops. There are so many mind-blowing views around Gertrude's Nose they actually become ho-hum after awhile.

Take heed of the red blazes - when they lead inland they are taking your dog away from potentially dangerous crevices in the Shawangunk conglomerate. An occasional rock scramble adds interest to your dog's hiking day, regardless. Pine trees in all shapes and sizes decorate the clifftops. In fall the blueberry bushes turn a bright scarlet and mingle with the deep greens of the conifers to paint an unforgettable Yule-like canvas.

Multiple options close the 7.5-mile loop; your dog will vote for the one that leads back to Lake Minnewaska for a well-earned doggie dip at the conclusion of America's best canine hike.

As a young lawyer, 19th century Senator George Graham Vest of Missouri, addressed the jury on behalf of his client, suing a neighbor who had killed his dog. Vest's speech has come to be known as "Tribute to the Dog."

The best friend a man has in the world may turn against him and become his enemy. His son or daughter that he has reared with loving care may prove ungrateful. Those who are nearest and dearest to us, those whom we trust with our happiness and our good name may become traitors to their faith. The money that a man has, he may lose. It flies away from him, perhaps when he needs it most. A man's reputation may be sacrificed in a moment of ill-considered action. The people who are prone to fall on their knees to do us honor when success is with us may be the first to throw the stone of malice when failure settles its cloud upon our heads. The one absolutely unselfish friend that man can have in this selfish world, the one that never deserts him, the one that never proves ungrateful or treacherous is his dog. A man's dog stands by him in prosperity and in poverty, in health and in sickness. He will sleep on the cold ground, where the wintry winds blow and the snow drives fiercely, if only he may be near his master's side. He will kiss the hand that has no food to offer; he will lick the wounds and sores that come in an encounter with the roughness of the world. He guards the sleep of his pauper master as if he were a prince. When all other friends desert, he remains. When riches take wings, and reputation falls to pieces, he is as constant in his love as the sun in its journey through the heavens. If fortune drives the master forth an outcast in the world, friendless and homeless, the faithful dog asks no higher privilege than that of accompanying him, to guard him against danger, to fight against his enemies. And when the last scene of all comes, and death takes his master in its embrace and his body is laid away in the cold ground, no matter if all other friends pursue their way, there by the graveside will the noble dog be found, his head between his paws, his eyes sad, but open in alert watchfulness, faithful and true even in death.

"If there are no dogs in Heaven,
then when I die I want to go where they went."
-Anonymous

Thanks for Attending The Waggies...

...You may also enjoy these other books on special places to hike with your dogs...

- 300 Day Hikes To Take With Your Dog Before He Tires You Out: Trails where you won't be able to wipe the wag off your dog's tail

- How To Hike With Dogs At Our National Parks - Even When They're Not Allowed On The Trail

www.ingramcontent.com/pod-product-compliance
Lightning Source LLC
Chambersburg PA
CBHW081149040426
42445CB00015B/1806